Object-Oriented
Rapid Prototyping

ANDREWS AND LEVENTHAL Fusion: Integrating IE, CASE, and JAD
ANDREWS AND STALICK Business Reengineering: The Survival Guide
AUGUST Joint Application Design
BLOCK The Politics of Projects
BODDIE The Information Asset: Rational DP Funding and Other Radical Notions
BOULDIN Agents of Change: Managing the Introduction of Automated Tools
BRILL Building Controls into Structured Systems
CHANG Principles of Visual Programming Systems
COAD AND NICOLA Object-Oriented Programming
COAD AND YOURDON Object-Oriented Analysis, 2/E
COAD AND YOURDON Object-Oriented Design
CONNELL AND SHAFER Object-Oriented Rapid Prototyping
CONNELL AND SHAFER Structured Rapid Prototyping
CONSTANTINE AND YOURDON Structured Design
CRAWFORD Advancing Business Concepts in a JAD Workshop Setting
DeGRACE AND STAHL The Olduvai Imperative: CASE and the State of Software
      Engineering Practice
DeGRACE AND STAHL Wicked Problems, Righteous Solutions
DeMARCO Controlling Software Projects
DeMARCO Structured Analysis and System Specification
EMBLEY, KURTZ, AND WOODFIELD Object-Oriented Systems Analysis
FOURNIER Practical Guide to Structured System Development and Maintenance
GLASS Software Conflict: Essays on the Art and Science of Software Engineering
JONES Assessment and Control of Software Risks
KING Project Management Made Simple
LARSON Interactive Software: Tools for Building Interactive User Interfaces
McMENAMIN AND PALMER Essential System Design
MOSLEY The Handbook of MIS Application Software Testing
PAGE-JONES Practical Guide to Structured Systems Design, 2/E
PINSON Designing Screen Interfaces in C
PUTNAM AND MYERS Measures for Excellence: Reliable Software on Time, within Budget
RIPPS An Implementation Guide to Real-Time Programming
RODGERS ORACLE®: A Database Developer's Guide
RODGERS UNIX®: Database Management Systems
SHLAER AND MELLOR Object Lifecycles: Modeling the World in States
SHLAER and MELLOR Object-Oriented Systems Analysis: Modeling the World in Data
SHILLER Software Excellence
THOMSETT Third Wave Project Management
WANG (ed.) Information Technology in Action
WARD System Development Without Pain
WARD AND MELLOR Structured Development for Real-Time Systems
YOURDON Decline and Fall of the American Programmer
YOURDON Managing the Structured Techniques 4/E
YOURDON Managing the System Life-Cycle, 2/E
YOURDON Modern Structured Analysis
YOURDON Object-Oriented Systems Design
YOURDON Structured Walkthroughs, 4/E
YOURDON Techniques of Program Structure and Design
YOURDON INC. YOURDON® Systems Method: Model-Driven Systems Development

Object-Oriented Rapid Prototyping

John L. Connell
Linda I. Shafer

YOURDON PRESS
Prentice Hall Building
Englewood Cliffs, New Jersey 07632

Library of Congress Cataloging-in-Publication Data

Connell, John L.
    Object-oriented rapid prototyping   /   John L. Connell, Linda
    I.   Shafer.
        p.   cm.
    Includes index.
    ISBN 0-13-629643-2
    1. Object-oriented programming (Computer science)   I. Shafer,
Linda,   II. Title.
QA76.64.C637   1995
005.1'1—dc20   94-5264
                                                                           CIP

Acquisitions editor: Paul Becker
Cover designer: Wanda Lubelski
Manufacturing manager: Alexis R. Heydt
Compositor/Production services: Pine Tree Composition, Inc.

©1995 by Prentice Hall P T R
Prentice-Hall, Inc.
A Simon & Schuster Company
Englewood Cliffs, New Jersey 07632

The publisher offers discounts on this book when ordered in bulk quantities.
For more information, contact:
                Corporate Sales Department
                Prentice Hall PTR
                113 Sylvan Avenue
                Englewood Cliffs, NJ 07632
                Phone: 201-592-2863
                FAX: 201-592-2249

Printed in the United States of America
10 9 8 7 6 5 4 3 2 1

ISBN 0-13-629643-2

Prentice-Hall International (UK) Limited, *London*
Prentice-Hall of Australia Pty. Limited, *Sydney*
Prentice-Hall Canada, Inc., *Toronto*
Prentice-Hall Hispoamericana, S.A., *Mexico*
Prentice-Hall of India Private Limited, *New Delhi*
Prentice-Hall of Japan, Inc., *Tokyo*
Simon & Schuster Asia Pte. Ltd., *Singapore*
Editora Prentice-Hall do Brasil, Ltda. *Rio de Janeiro*

Contents

Preface

In the 1980s, we were assured by pundits that structured methods, CASE tools, information engineering, and RAD approaches could improve software development productivity dramatically. While those tools did increase productivity in some situations, the magnitude of improvement industry-wide was disappointing. Current literature now promises that the silver bullets for improving productivity are object-oriented methods and the automated tools and languages that support those methods.

As of this writing, we have reason to be optimistic about the object-oriented approach. We do not feel that the 1980s techniques were *bad*. They solved many quality problems and provided some productivity advantages. Object-oriented tools and techniques are better, however; they will solve more problems and provide much greater improvement in productivity.

It is now possible for a very small self-managed team of object-oriented rapid prototypers to accomplish in several months a task that used to take several years with many software engineers and several layers of management. Object-oriented tools and techniques have contributed to this productivity gain in three fundamental ways:

- Object-oriented developers seem to typically operate in a concurrent, iterative, incremental fashion, practicing rapid prototyping as a natural part of the development process and thereby gaining insight into true functional requirements earlier in the development process;
- Object-oriented development tools and methods are more powerful in terms of their ability to deliver units of functionality per unit of effort, because the syntax of the tools and the

notation of the methods implement functionality equivalent to procedural languages and notations with a fraction of the amount of effort.

- For object-oriented software, reuse is enhanced by change resilience (encapsulation) and change automation (inheritance), and is therefore more widely practiced.

Conservatives, observing of the rush to object-oriented technology, often register concern over the sudden death of structured techniques and the sequential lifecycle. Didn't they serve us well? Won't software developers regress back to the hacking approaches of the 1960s? Doesn't the lack of formal methods produce undocumented, unmaintainable, spaghetti code and erode overall productivity? These conservative questions are not without merit, but there is no turning back. Object-oriented methods have proven their potential and are here to stay. But you do not have to make a choice between object-oriented approaches and rapid prototyping on one side, and rigorous methods and quality software on the other. This book is not about hacking, nor is it about overspecification. It is about balance, explaining how the object-oriented rapid prototyper can walk the high middle ground, producing high-quality, clearly documented, easily maintainable software that provides the highest possible user satisfaction with minimum total effort.

This book provides a how-to approach to object-oriented rapid prototyping, providing a realistic look at how object-oriented methods and tools may be applied in an iterative prototyping lifecycle. The step by step tutorial contained in Chapters 5, 6, and 7 provides directions for developing, iterating, refining, and evolving a prototype into a deliverable software application. Start reading there if you're anxious to dive right into the how-to specifics and feel you are already comfortable with the basics of prototyping and object-oriented methods.

Chapter 5 shows how to use object-oriented analysis and design approaches to produce a graphic model of the application, and then develop a demonstrable prototype based on the model. In Chapter 6, prototype iteration is explained in detail. The user-developer feedback/iterate loop is described, both in terms of how it works and how it is controlled. Chapter 7 tells how to turn a user-approved prototype into a deliverable software application without throwing the prototype away and starting over. Software developed using this approch is very satisfying to customers as they can see immediate and sustained results.

The three tutorial chapters are crucial, but not sufficient. Before they will make sense, most readers will need to have an understanding of what rapid prototyping really is (as opposed to the folklore of rapid prototyping), why it should be object-oriented, how specification methods benefit rapid prototyping, and what kinds of advanced development tools are critical for optimal rapid prototyping. Chapters 1 through 4 provide a fast track to rapid prototyping and object-oriented methods, condensing many ideas into one foundation.

Beginning with Chapter 8, there are several chapters that you will find helpful as you undertake the application of these methods to an actual development project. Techniques are suggested for tailoring a conventional lifecycle, managing new kinds of risks, estimating and measuring productivity in a new object-oriented way, applying CASE tools, and getting started using this new approach. These chapters will take you beyond simply knowing how to practice a new technique, you will also learn how to make the technique produce successful results on real projects.

This book is not a programming guide for object-oriented languages such as C++ and Smalltalk. It is a guide for understanding and practicing a new development paradigm with roots in powerful analysis and design modeling techniques. We feel the software engineering community is poised to accept guidelines for quieting the disruption created by a totally new development paradigm. The synergism of formal analysis and design methods combined with rapid prototyping is more feasible with object-oriented techniques than with previous approaches.

Many object-oriented programmers we have talked to are beginning to have a deeper understanding that it is difficult to code good classes of objects without a thorough understanding of formal object-oriented design principles. On the formalist side, leading object-oriented methodologists such as Peter Coad, Ed Yourdon, Ivar Jacobson, Ian Graham, Rebecca Wirfs-Brock, and Adele Goldberg have all insisted in their writings that object-oriented specifications will not be accurate unless a lot of iterative prototyping is done concurrently during requirements definition. It is obvious that a meeting of the minds between practitioners and methodologists is happening. Object-oriented rapid prototyping is the process wherein methodology and programming meet and function together smoothly.

Instead of tacking a thin veneer of prototyping onto the tail end of object-oriented specification methods, we take just the opposite approach. The proven technique of formalized rapid prototyping serves as the framework into which the new object-oriented analysis and design models are slipped.

The original goal of rapid prototyping is unchanged: accurately reflecting user feedback while evolving the developing prototype to a high-quality maintainable system that meets the users' needs. Only the vehicle used to traverse the path is new. The structured, procedural, hierarchical, function-oriented development tools and modeling approaches have been replaced with object-oriented, message-driven, encapsulated, change-resilient, data-oriented tools and modeling approaches. In doing so, vast improvements are made, providing dynamic requirements models that

- more accurately reflect the real world;
- provide the best way to leverage reuse of existing software components in the development of new prototypes and applications;
- reduce long-term system expenses by narrowing the focus of maintenance effort to the component level.

You have a choice: the conservative drudgery of total prespecification with customer signoff before coding, the joyous but dangerous practice of prototyping without specifications, or a concurrent engineering approach undertaking both specification and implementation at the same time. The concurrent engineering approach produces the best results more often and is more feasible with object-oriented technology. Well-designed object classes are more resuable in new prototypes than procedural programs. Object-oriented specification methods do not get in the way with rapid prototyping—they provide assistance. Modern object-oriented rapid prototyping tools are more robust than the 4GLs, relational databases, and other prototyping tools of the 1980s.

With object-oriented technology, no one can effectively argue that reuse and rapid prototyping are concepts that don't work. Object-oriented developers don't write monolithic procedural programs; they write reusable object classes. They don't create tedious and error-prone prespecification; they do concurrent, incremental, object-oriented analysis, design, development, and testing.

Although there are now few arguments about the validity of

rapid prototyping as a requirements discovery approach, there are still few published descriptions of exactly what that means or how to do it. How do developers go about performing the necessary activities? The authors have had more than a decade of experience on dozens of successful rapid prototyping projects. This is our second book on the subject. We have distilled our experience into a step-by-step formalization of the object-oriented rapid prototyping approach. We are successfully using this approach currently on several projects. We hope our real-world experience will help you to achieve a faster assimilation of object-oriented rapid prototyping in your environment. We firmly believe that object-oriented rapid analysis and design performed concurrently with iterative prototyping is not just theory: It really works!

We thank Nancy, Don, Jason, Leslie, Bree, Sterling Software, NASA Ames, and Sterling Information Group.

John L. Connell
Linda I. Shafer

Object-Oriented
Rapid Prototyping

1
Basics

Rapid prototyping has been in common use on software development projects for some time. It is primarily a requirements discovery technique, used to help determine the application functionality, data structure, and control characteristics of a system. User requirements are explored through experimental development, demonstration, refinement, and iteration. In a previous text, *Structured Rapid Prototyping*,[1] rapid prototyping was differentiated from *hacking* (developing conventional software programs without benefit of formal requirements or design specification), and *prespecification* (presupposing and baselining detailed requirements and design specifications before developing any software).

The formalized approach presented in *Structured Rapid Prototyping* assumed a middle ground: concurrent software engineering using formal analysis and design methods—specify a little, develop a little, demonstrate, iterate. Paper documents representing requirements and design are static and passive, but a software rapid prototype is a dynamic, interactive, visual model of the user's requirements as an implemented design. The prototype provides a basis for dialog between developers and users that is far more effective than either text or static models.

A useful rapid prototype has the following characteristics:

- It is built quickly and demonstrated early
- It provides mechanisms for users to try out proposed parts of a system, and then give direction for additional features and refinement
- It is easy to modify
- It is initially intentionally incomplete

This book is a combination of formalized rapid prototyping methods, object-oriented analysis and design methods, and documented experiences from many rapid prototyping projects. It will describe how specification and prototype iteration can exist in a symbiotic and synergistic relationship. Productivity gains and software quality, improved with rapid prototyping, may be further improved with object-oriented rapid prototyping. Before launching into an explanation of how to do object-oriented rapid prototyping, the following typical concerns about the feasibility of this approach are addressed.

RAPID PROTOTYPING—STILL NEEDED
FOR REQUIREMENTS MODELING

Rapid prototyping is still necessary for requirements specification, even though the object-oriented paradigm is an improvement. If users knew precisely what their requirements were at the start of development projects, and if developers were perfectly skilled at understanding the users' statements of requirements and translating them into software specifications, then we would need only good static modeling paradigms. The truth is that object-oriented analysis and design may be correctly applied, and yet the delivered software may still fail to meet users' real requirements. Object-oriented rapid prototyping is a way to leverage the power of rapid prototyping for requirements gathering by coupling it with improved real-world modeling made possible with objects.

Figure 1.1 shows the universe of prespecified requirements as being very out-of-sync with the universe of users' real requirements. Software built to presupposed requirements will have to be reworked after delivery to the user. Our observation is that the extent to which this happens, and will probably always happen, is significant.

Figure 1.1 also suggests an alternative to expensive post-delivery rework: Perform *rapid analysis* (incomplete, using graphic models) of the tiny area of most probable overlap between presupposed requirements and real requirements (the area containing requirements of which we are certain); then build a *prototype* to this intentionally incomplete specification; and then proceed with requirements definition through iterative discovery.

Thus, rapid prototyping does not replace object-oriented analy-

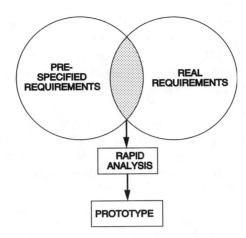

Figure 1.1: The alternative to prespecification

sis (OOA); it is something you would do to as the first step of OOA. This is consistent with many OOA approaches, for example, Coad and Yourdon, wherein rapid prototyping is referred to repeatedly as a required technique for augmenting requirements definition.[2]

OBJECT-ORIENTED RAPID PROTOTYPING— AN IMPROVED APPROACH

In the history of software engineering, we have consistently built upon methods that work for us, reusing, rather than replacing them. Structured programming from the 1960s is still relevant today. Structured design from the early 1970s is also still widely used, as is structured analysis from the late 1970s and early 1980s. In the evolution of structured techniques, improvements to the software development process simply added new techniques to the established base. We began to move backwards through the conceptual development lifecycle.

A typical lifecycle finds analysis activities followed by design activities, and design followed by coding. The software engineering industry reversed this order and attacked coding problems first with structured programming techniques. When improved coding failed to solve all quality problems, design was improved with structure charts and other structured design techniques,[3] but structured programming continued to be used. The third major movement toward amending the lifecycle process was structured analysis[4] (data flow diagrams, entity-relationship diagrams), while structured design and structured programming continued to be used in phases following analysis. Rapid prototyping, the fourth major technique applied, is employed even earlier in the lifecycle, before requirements are baselined, and continues to exercise all of the previous techniques.

The advent of object-oriented rapid prototyping provides a mixture of proven techniques along with new ones. Some of the analysis, design, and development methods will necessarily change to employ the power of objects, and those changes will be fully described here.

You may not need convincing that rapid prototyping is necessary for building correct software, but you may be wondering what it means for rapid prototyping to be object-oriented and whether the object-orientation is necessary. Does it mean prototyping objects? Does it imply the use of object-oriented programming languages?

When rapid prototyping was *structured* rather than *object-oriented*, we recommended use of structured analysis in a concurrent engineering approach with rapid prototype development and iteration. The prototype and the requirements specification evolved together. The tools of the specifier included dataflow diagrams and entity-relationship diagrams. The tools of the prototyper included fourth generation languages, visual programming environments, and flexible data management systems.

This book recommends the application of object-oriented tools and techniques to the same type of concurrent software engineering approach. The OOA/OOD specification and the object-oriented prototype should evolve together as shown in Figure 1.2. The tools, however, are changed. The tools of the OO analyst/designer are OO models. The tools of OO prototyper include very high productivity OO development environments, reusable object class libraries, and flexible object-oriented data management systems. So what was wrong with the structured rapid prototyping approach that it needed to be abandoned? Nothing, really, and the useful portions are actually reused, not abandoned. Every time it has been applied correctly, it has produced successful results. We see object-oriented techniques as an opportunity to improve an already successful approach rather than fixing an approach that didn't quite work. For instance, the following opportunities for improvement can be exploited by moving to an object-oriented paradigm:

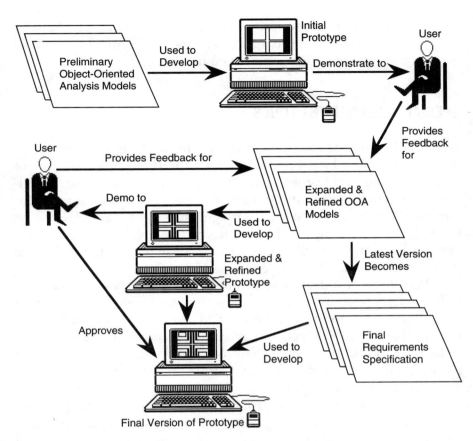

Figure 1.2: Iterating the specification with the prototype

- OOA, OOD, and object-oriented development environments allow for modeling the real world of the user's problem space rather than the world of software processes and dataflows;
- The models of OOA and OOD are more in sync with each other than were the models of structured analysis and structured design (SA/SD);
- There are no activities analogous to the transform analysis or transaction analysis that were needed to translate structured analysis DFDs into structured design structure charts, thereby reducing the number of overall steps in the process;
- The OOA and OOD models will be more in sync with object-oriented prototypes than SA/SD models were with their related prototypes;

- At last the true promise of powerfully practical reuse can be fully realized (due to special capabilities found within most object-oriented development environments).

SPECIAL DEVELOPMENT TOOLS

Good tools are at the very heart of any form of rapid prototyping, and particularly object-oriented rapid prototyping. Some form of object-oriented rapid prototyping can be accomplished in any development environment, but the difference between working in a conventional environment with languages such as C, FORTRAN, or COBOL, and working in a highly productive object-oriented development environment with power tools can make a huge difference in productivity and effectiveness.

Poor tools result in slow prototyping. Not only do prototypes produced without power tools take longer to develop, they are also more difficult to modify and iterate. The result can be a development project that is prohibitively expensive, particularly if the specifications are evolved along with the prototype. If the specifications are not evolved, then the development effort can be viewed as hacking rather than rapid prototyping.

The best object-oriented prototyping development environment consists of tools that are both good prototyping tools (quick to build, easy to modify) in addition to being very object-oriented. These two characteristics are, unfortunately, not always mutually present. Just because a language or a data management system is object-oriented, does not mean that it necessarily provides the best prototyping environment. Because proper tool selection is so critical to the success of a rapid prototyping project, future chapters will delve into this issue in detail.

EVOLUTION OF OBJECT-ORIENTED RAPID PROTOTYPES INTO DELIVERABLE SOFTWARE

Object-oriented prototypes can be leveraged into production in many cases. Will the target environment host the tool used to develop and evolve the prototype (or any good prototyping tool)? If not, it still makes sense to prototype; just count on starting over once requirements are finalized. While starting over sounds expensive, it actually adds only about 10 percent to the cost of a conventional pre-specified build, and will produce a final product that is twice as good. Evolutionary prototyping is the ideal, because prototype components surviving in the final product provide building blocks for requested modifications. With good tools, object-oriented rapid prototyping techniques can be applied throughout the entire life of a software product, including the post-implementation phase.

APPLICATION TYPES MOST SUITABLE
FOR OBJECT-ORIENTED RAPID PROTOTYPING

Virtually any application is a good candidate for this approach. Real-time embedded systems without strong user interfaces should not be excluded. They may present some unique challenges, but the authors have found prototyping to be enormously useful for many such systems. Every new application will have certain problem areas that will cause the developer to worry, "How can I prototype this?" Such difficulties can almost always be overcome. Examples of creative prototyping strategies are given throughout this book to help you.

COMPATIBILITY WITH OOA
AND OOD SPECIFICATION TECHNIQUES

The news here is very good indeed. Rapid prototyping is much enhanced by the concurrent application of object-oriented analysis and design techniques. This is a book about object-oriented software engineering. Contained herein is a methodology for software development that combines the best of the object-oriented analysis, object-oriented design, and object-oriented development techniques. The approach alters the lifecycle to accommodate the development, demonstration, and refinement of a working model during the analysis phase of a project to define the true and complete set of software requirements.

Object-oriented analysis and *structured rapid prototyping* are two of the more recent additions to a family of closely related requirements analysis approaches. *Object-oriented rapid prototyping* is the most recent addition to this family. All family members recommend graphical representations of requirements; many of the graphics notational conventions are much the same from one requirements methodology to another. The move from structured rapid prototyping to object-oriented rapid prototyping is not difficult, and it yields tremendous benefits.

EXTENT OF END USER INVOLVEMENT

Without fully involved and participating users, it simply isn't possible to have a successful rapid prototyping project. The term *user* is open to various interpretations. Subsequent chapters will broadly define who the users are for an OORP project and suggest a more precise term—*requirements commissioners*. Prototype demonstration and iteration are the mechanisms for the discovery of what sorts of objects are of interest to the commissioners, what they want to know about those objects, how they want to control them, and how they want them to behave.

The commissioner's role need not be limited solely to passively viewing and critiquing the prototype. Some of the better object-oriented prototyping tools are very easy to learn and use. Experience has shown that rapid prototyping is most effectively performed by teams of professional developers and requirements commissioners working side by side toward the same goals.

COST REDUCTION AND RISK MITIGATION BENEFITS

Rapid prototyping intends to reduce the risk of high cost and poor quality through the efficient discovery and implementation of true requirements. Cost is reduced over the life of the product, because fewer changes will be necessary after it is delivered, when it is most expensive to change. Rapid prototyping was not intended to reduce development time as the primary goal. The term *rapid* is a reference to the timeframe in which a user sees preliminary results.

Developers do not spend the majority of their effort on coding. Much development effort is spent on producing documents: management plans, concept documents, requirements specifications, design documents, test plans, user guides, and others. Rapid prototyping does not provide justification for eliminating these documents; short cuts are not advised. Object-oriented rapid prototyping is not a quick and dirty approach. It complements and augments existing object-oriented analysis and design specification techniques, rather than replacing them.

Software costs can be dramatically reduced, however, because prototyping serves to help surface and correct problems in the very early stages of development, before too many components need to be reworked. Modifying a prototype is quick, easy, and painless—if the right tools are in use. The types of errors best caught by prototyping are also the ones that will be most costly to correct—those that involve delivering the wrong features to the user and failing to deliver the right ones. Incorrect, inconsistent, ambiguous, and incomplete requirements specifications are still produced on many projects (even using object-oriented analysis), which results in software that is not what the user wanted. Properly implemented rapid prototyping can significantly shorten development time, even though that is not the primary goal, and will result in dramatic savings in total lifecycle costs because it meets the user's needs.

Without rapid prototyping, software is often produced that does not provide information expected by the user, or it provides information that is extremely difficult to use, is in undecipherable formats, or is inaccurate. The resulting loss of efficiency and productivity on the part of the user is the hidden cost of conventionally developed software. Rapid prototyping creates software with the right features and the correct information processing, because prototype users have been able to experiment with iterations of incremental versions of a working model of the system throughout the life of the development project. Continual refinements and enhancements are encouraged, as opposed to freezing requirements after specifications have been signed off, before coding starts. On rapid prototyping projects, valid requirements are sometimes discovered during prototype demonstrations near the end of the iterative prototype refinement phase—to the pleasant surprise of the users.

The specific benefits of rapid prototyping can include:

- Obtaining reliable feedback from users on required user interface and system output features
- Discovering detailed requirements for data storage, processing functionality, and system control or behavior

- Discovering and helping to develop solutions to performance problems
- Reducing development costs
- Providing proof of a concept or feasibility
- Providing a method for developing deliverable software that optimally meets the true needs of the user, thereby vastly reducing maintenance costs while increasing user productivity

THE RISKS OF RAPID PROTOTYPING

Rapid prototyping does not introduce any new political, economic, or technical risks to the software development process. It is a risk reduction technique, as discussed above. Things do, however, go wrong with some rapid prototyping projects, often because of poor understanding of the procedural differences between rapid prototyping and conventional software development. Chapter 8 describes many of these dangers and provides suggestions for assuring success. Things can go wrong on rapid prototyping projects:

- operating on the basis of mistaken concepts regarding definitions, objectives, and techniques
- disagreeing about methodologies, standards, and tools
- being unable to control users who want to iterate and evolve a prototype beyond the scope of budget and schedule
- taking quality short-cuts rationalized by misuse of the term *rapid prototyping*
- delivering a prototype prematurely instead of a final (thoroughly documented and performance-tuned) product
- over-engineering prototypes that emphasize performance and design elegance over modifiability
- not providing training for maintenance personnel

Education provides the solutions to these problems. Attempting an object-oriented rapid prototyping project when the participants do not agree on definitions, methodologies, tools, techniques, and procedures often leads to failure. This book recommends and describes a project plan which should be used at project startup to define these elements and provide an understanding between users and developers as to responsibilities and deliverables. The plan can be used during the project to assist in convergence toward a solution during prototype iteration, to prevent quality shortcuts, and to head off premature delivery of the software.

THE FUTURE OF OBJECT-ORIENTED RAPID PROTOTYPING

Rapid prototyping, introduced more than ten years ago, has proven that it is here to stay. Object-oriented software engineering in general, and object-oriented rapid prototyping specifically, are also expected to be increasingly popular and permanent. These powerful new approaches to software development are now beginning to be used in many organizations for the development of many new, large, complex applications. Tools required for a proper job of object-oriented rapid prototyping have been introduced with much greater frequency in the last few years. Dramatic improvements in the capabilities provided by such tools continue to appear in new releases. The effort that vendors are putting into high level object-oriented development environment tools is a response to the market demand. New product development is one way to tell that object-oriented rapid prototyping is where the action is.

Rapid prototyping has been practiced since the early 1980s and has become standard operating procedure in most successful software development organizations. The typical software development shop has at the very least modified the conventional lifecycle approach to include iteration, place less reliance on paper products for analysis and design, and use high level development tools, such as fourth generation languages, for prototyping.

However, those changes have produced mixed results. In some organizations, prototype-developed software has exhibited a distinct tendency to satisfy true user requirements better and produce information and functionality that is more complete, more accurate, and more meaningful. In others, a formalized, successfully repeatable approach to rapid prototyping was not used and the results were often disastrous. Just because it's fast and just because it's iterative, does not mean it's wonderful!

Object-oriented rapid prototyping (OORP) is a formalized approach and has proven to be successfully repeatable, just as *structured rapid prototyping* was. In the future, OORP will become a mainstream approach to developing new software because it produces even better systems at even lower cost than the structured approach.

ENDNOTES

1. Connell, J., and Shafer, L., *Structured Rapid Prototyping*. Englewood Cliffs, NJ: Prentice-Hall, Inc. 1989.

2. Coad, P., and Yourdon, E., *Object-Oriented Analysis*. Englewood Cliffs, NJ: Prentice-Hall, Inc. 1991.

3. Constantine, L., and Yourdon, E., *Structured Design*. Englewood Cliffs, NJ: Prentice-Hall, Inc. 1975.

4. DeMarco, T., *Structured Analysis and System Specification*, New York: Yourdon Press, 1983.

2

Terms

There seem to be no universally agreed upon definitions of the terms *object-oriented* and *rapid prototyping*. This chapter offers working definitions of these and other commonly misunderstood terms so that we can have a meaningful dialogue based on a common language.

THE LEGACY DEFINITION OF SOFTWARE RAPID PROTOTYPING

Many developers have their own experience-based definition—something they have done and thought of as rapid prototyping. Although such approaches may have worked well for those individuals, they may not have been formalized and published, and thus may not be repeatable for others. These home grown definitions take many forms and imply very different types of activities. As published, the term rapid prototyping has taken on a more uniform standard definition involving using easy-to-modify software models to discover application requirements.

Beware of misconceptions arising from misuse of the word rapid. *Rapid* implies development cost savings. If, however, prototype development and iteration is something done *in addition to* requirements specification, design specification, final implementation coding, testing, and other conventional development activities, total development costs may be higher than without prototyping. This is not necessarily inappropriate, since the primary objective is to use rapid prototyping to help build and deliver the right system, not solely to cut development costs.

In hardware engineering, *prototype* usually refers to a fully designed system model that will undergo final testing before being mass produced. In software, we simply call that *testing,* and prototyping is an activity usually begun well before the final design is complete, in order to discover and validate requirements.

The primary purpose of a software prototype is to help users determine what things the software should do and how it should do them. Without prototyping, the users have to trust their software developers to develop and deliver systems that are easy to use, fill their needs, help them to be more professional at their jobs, and will be available in time to meet their needs. Prototyping provides users with a way to become directly and interactively involved in the design and development of their software and be less dependent on the complexities of human communications.

Rapid prototyping is user-driven dynamic requirements modeling—a mouthful, but a phrase with clarity. A popular alternative phrase, *rapid application development* (RAD), does not evoke formalisms; it could be accomplished by getting developers to work lots of unpaid overtime.

Conventional requirements modeling means that a specification is written and signed off on by the users before proceeding with development. Dynamic requirements modeling means that an operational software model is developed and demonstrated to users in order to produce additional requirements and verify the correctness of the implemented ones.

A SHORT HISTORY OF RAPID PROTOTYPING

In the 1970s, there were no prototyping tools, and rapid prototyping was not a very good idea. Software programs can easily be inflexible and difficult to understand and change when built with low-level languages. This is why the early structured analysts advocated getting the dataflow diagrams right before proceeding any further with development. The idea was that dataflow diagrams are easier for users to review and developers to modify than FORTRAN or COBOL source code. This is still a correct notion, so don't develop requirements prototypes in FORTRAN or COBOL (or any other third generation language)!

The rules changed when good prototyping tools made prototypes as easy to modify as analysis and design diagrams. Certainly, no one can effectively argue today that diagrams are easier for users to review than prototypes built with advanced tools. Ask users what they think about this. By the mid-1980s, screen formatters, program generators, report generators, fourth generation languages, and relational databases provided prototypers with industrial-strength capability to rapidly modify data storage structures interactively; to create, demonstrate, and modify prototype features using menus and screen forms that minimized programming effort; and often to evolve the resulting prototype into a deliverable production system.

The following are characteristics of a good software prototype:

- It's functional quickly
- It's a model
- It's easy to modify
- It really works
- It's developed with advanced prototyping tools
- It focuses on the human interfaces
- It promotes communication between developers and users
- It is used to discover requirements

Structured rapid prototyping rephrases those characteristics by defining a rapid prototype as an easily modifiable and extensible working model of a proposed system, not necessarily representative of a complete system, which provides users of the application with a physical representation of key parts of the system before implementation; and an easily built, readily modifiable, ultimately extensible, partially specified, working model of the primary aspects of a proposed system.

RISKY DEFINITIONS OF SOFTWARE PROTOTYPING

There are divergent philosophies regarding how to accomplish rapid prototyping. Some of these produce suboptimal results. The most common of the suboptimal approaches can be labeled *pretty screens*, *only-a-model*, *overengineered*, and *hacking*.

Pretty Screens

This is a very old and still prevalent approach to prototyping. It is an inexpensive, low-risk way to get your feet wet by doing a little prototyping of the appearance of a few screens for the users. Special training on the use of exotic new tools will not be necessary. Some appropriate tools for prototyping pretty screens include a number two pencil, crayons, an etch-a-sketch toy, and a personal computer graphics drawing software package.

Screens are shown to the user and modified until pleasing; then the real screens are programmed to match.

User approval of such a prototype does not constitute any kind of meaningful requirements definition. The pretty screens approach will enhance user satisfaction with the final product, but it will not help to discover required application objects, behavior, data structure, or control mechanisms. Dynamic prototypes offer the user an opportunity to experiment with these factors interactively, while viewing familiar data being manipulated. Evaluating the prettiness of a screen will not reveal whether the information shown on the screen is easy to obtain, accurate, sufficient, or intelligible.

Only-a-Model Prototypes

With this approach, prototypes are used only to help identify requirements during the analysis phase of a development project. The prototype is built using an advanced development environment suitable for a quick build and rapid modifications. After requirements are finalized, programming starts over from scratch using the real implementation language on the target machine. Only-a-model prototyping may not save much money in development costs, but it still provides the same benefit of reducing enhancement costs during the maintenance phase because the right requirements will be implemented.

This approach, as with pretty screen prototyping, is often forced on developers who lack industrial-strength prototyping tools or do not have access to the target hardware. Tools that are suitable only for building nondeliverable prototypes may be characterized by having lackluster performance and no capability of integrating other software. Development environments that do not produce software with good performance characteristics and that do not allow the substitution of lower-level language programs for poorly performing prototype code cannot be used effectively for evolutionary prototyping. When circumstances dictate availability of a good prototyping tool on a development machine, no prototyping tools on the target computer, and no possibility of cross platform portability, then only-a-model is a good use of the prototyping approach.

Since characteristics of the prototyping tools used are the difference between only-a-model and evolutionary prototypes, it makes sense to get good tools and do the latter. The cost of good tools is typically less than the cost of total reprogramming after requirements definition, particularly since one tool can be used for many projects. Some factors that get in the way of acquisition of good tools are procurement constraints, organizational politics, and hardware preferences. If you have to live with these kinds of nontechnical constraints, prototypes that are only-a-model are much better than no prototypes at all.

Overengineered Prototypes

This approach is used by people who are not comfortable with producing software prior to fully specified requirements and a completely defined design. A prototype is shown to users shortly before final delivery only to make sure that nothing has been overlooked. Major changes are often requested, but usually strongly resisted on the grounds that the prototype meets approved specifications. Errors and minor defects are corrected before the system is delivered. This can hardly be called dynamic requirements discovery. With the overengineered prototyping approach, requirements are defined using conventional interviewing and static modeling techniques.

It is not good to resist user-requested changes simply because they are inconsistent with a user-approved paper specification. Users frequently approve paper specifications out of frustration with the lengthy specification process and lack of comprehensibility of the resulting product. Specification signoff usually comes down to whether or not users trust their developers (experience teaches them they should not).

Often, developers of overengineered prototypes offer users the opportunity to incorporate major change requests into a phase two project after delivery of the current version of the software. This is a big waste of time and money because it usually means that major portions of the old requirements and design documents, as well as the prototype, must be rewritten. The smart rapid prototyper avoids specifying features when not very certain of necessity or correct implementation.

Cocky managers of projects that have developed an overengineered prototype can often be heard bragging that their team has produced a really slick prototype that will really impress the users and *validate* the requirements document. Unfortunately, what prototypes do best is serve to *invalidate* prespecified requirements by uncovering all of the user-developer misunderstandings. This is a good thing if a large portion of your budget and schedule have not already been spent on specifications.

Hacking without Specifications

Sometimes rapid prototyping is used as an excuse for not doing any form of requirements or design specification, or at least an amount well below what is required for a high-quality, maintainable system. Under this approach, developers work hard, fast, and iteratively on the code alone, until they get it right. The user may or may not be asked to review the various evolving versions. It's rapid because they work really hard and because they escape the requirement to document because they're supposedly using a state-of-the-art rapid prototyping approach.

This approach used to be called hacking; calling it rapid prototyping does not improve the quality of the results. If conventional programming languages are used to produce the software (the usual case with hacking), modifying the programs many times during prototype iterations will eventually destroy any readability or understandability that was designed into the initial version. If design specifications are not produced first, the programs will probably not be easy to read and understand. For large and complex applications, modified many times during prototype iterations, the result will be someone's maintenance nightmare, even if that someone is the developer.

This approach is also often forced on developers by lack of good prototyping tools. At other times it is simply dictated by incompetent project management or users with too much power. Without tools that allow for a very quick build and very quick modifications, the prototyper must skimp on activities, other than coding, in order to qualify his or her prototyping approach as rapid. Specification is the obvious target for effort reduction.

Conventional programs are sometimes developed without documentation as prototypes, with the promise that they will be thrown away and rewritten from good specifications after user approval of the prototype. The problem is, the programs usually are not thrown away. It is too tempting not to implement functionality that has proven to be popular with users. Hasty specifications may be produced as an afterthought, but the system will still be difficult to maintain.

EVOLUTIONARY RAPID PROTOTYPING

Build something that really works and contains actual user-familiar data, instead of just a pretty-screens prototype. Build it with tools that allow for performance tuning through integration with other software, so that it is not just a requirements model and you will not have to start over again. Prespecify only the tiny portion of requirements for which you are very sure there is complete understanding and agreement between you and the users. Do so before initiating prototype development, so that the prototype will not be over-engineered and overly expensive to iterate. Do requirements and design specification in tiny increments before each prototype iteration to avoid hacking and to deliver maintainable software. Use an advanced prototyping toolkit so that all this can be accomplished in less time than a conventional build. This is evolutionary rapid prototyping.

OBJECT-ORIENTED SOFTWARE ENGINEERING

The following paragraphs will define terms that were introduced to the software engineering field with the advent of object-oriented techniques. Most of these terms—object, abstraction, encapsulation, inheritance, message—have commonly understood meanings in everyday speech. Their meaning in software engineering is similar, but those who are unfamiliar with object-oriented (OO) techniques may find the terms difficult to understand in a software context.

The OO terms encourage software developers not to think of software applications as hierarchical (top-down, functionally decomposed), but rather in terms of a flat set of interchangeable (and thus reusable) components. The terminology also encourages developers to think of applications as solutions to users' problems, rather than as solutions to a computer problem. Users want to know things about certain objects in their environment. They want to be able to control the behavior of certain objects. Users could care less about the hierarchy of functional decomposition in which one of their control processes is contained. Thus, the purpose of the OO terms is to encourage a paradigm shift.

Object Abstraction

What is an *object* in software? An object can be defined as a thing to which thought and action is directed. This definition is consistent with usage in everyday speech. A software object is an abstraction of a thing to which the thought and action of the software user is directed.

The creation of objects in software is accomplished through identification of *things* that the user is interested in for the purpose of the application at hand, and an abstraction of those real-world *things* into subsets of information about and behavior of them. For example, a type of real-world thing the user might be interested in could be employees. Employees have spouses, cars, religions, and shoe sizes. A software object instance could contain data about spouse's name, type of car, religion, and shoe size. But, for a particular application, the user might not care about these attributes. Instead, the user might want to know the employee's name, social security number, home and work telephone numbers, address, hourly rate, and department number. This collection of information about the object of interest to the user constitutes the appropriate abstraction of the real-world thing into a software object for a given application.

If the information about an employee in the above example were captured in a file or database table, then the record in that file or row in that database would be an *instance* of the employee *class* of objects. A real-world object class can be represented in software as a data abstraction, described by the attributes of the real-world object that are of interest to the user.

The Smalltalk and C++ object-oriented programming languages (OOPLs), and other OOPLs, use the word *class* to represent a generalized abstraction of a real-world object and then use the word *object* to represent a specific occurrence or instance of that class of object. In an OOPL, employee would be a class and the employee, Tom Smith, would be an object.

The approach of calling an object an object, rather than a class, seems more intuitive. If you want to refer to a particular class of object, say "the employee object class." If you want to talk about an instance, say "an instance of the employee object." This jargon prefer-

Real World	Smalltalk	C++	We say ...
Object	Class	Class	Object Class
Attribute	Attribute	Variable	Attribute
Process	Method	Function	Service
Occurrence	Object	Object	Object Instance
General/Subtype	Super/Sub Class	Base/Derived Class	Base/Derived Class
Control	Message	Message	Message

Figure 2.1: Object-oriented jargon mapping matrix

ence is not really important, but an understanding of the mapping is essential (see Figure 2.1).

Encapsulation of Data and Process

Encapsulation is a concept that, assisted by many object-oriented development environments, encourages the development of objects in such a way that they will be self-contained, having minimal interaction with other objects in the application. The goal of encapsulation is to make everything an object will need to provide the services it will render an integral part of the object. Software operations and the data they operate on are bound together, and the binding constitutes encapsulation. Direct access to that data by other objects in the system is discouraged.

Messages (defined below) are received by objects, and, upon receipt, the object provides the service that contains a handler for that message. Objects can communicate with each other using messages, and small amounts of data can be passed in a message, but one object does not care how another object performs its services, or what data is employed. Since this approach obviously supports concurrent processing and preprocessing functions, it can be much more efficient than hierarchical procedural software design.

The real value of encapsulation is productivity improvement during software maintenance and rapid prototyping, activities that involve lots of effort applied toward the modification of existing software. Well-encapsulated object classes are protected from the changes made to other object classes. When working with conventionally developed software, both software maintenance professionals and rapid prototypers fear the *ripple* effect—where changing a few lines of code will have negative effects on the integrity of many other pieces of code across the entire application system. Such interdependencies are extremely difficult to identify or prevent in hierarchically designed and developed software. With encapsulated software object classes, the integrity and autonomy of the code and data within every object class within the application is preserved throughout all modifications.

A fringe benefit of encapsulation is the reusability of well-encapsulated object classes. An object class that does not need much, if anything, in the way of data or services from other object classes, is going to be very easy to reuse in other applications. It does not contain assumptions about the environment or the architecture of the system in which it exists. A programmer interested in reusing such an object class does not have to be interested in the entire application problem space. Such an object class can become a part of any future prototype with little or no modification effort. It can be thought of as a *black box* component whose services can be trusted and are instantaneously available.

Inheritance Structures

Inheritance is a concept that, assisted by object-oriented development environments, provides the capability to develop new object classes by simply extending the structure of previously built object classes. The extensions can consist of added attributes and/or added services. The object classes created using this approach are part of an inheritance structure where they are children or derived classes of the object from which they were created. The parent object class passed its services and attributes on to the child object classes, which added their own unique services and attributes.

If, for example a ship is an object class, a sailboat is one type of ship, a powerboat is another, a yacht is another, and a dinghy is yet another type. All of these types of ships can be derived object classes of the base ship object class. The user may want to know certain kinds of information about all ships, such as the ship's name, owner's name, owner's phone number, and owner's address. If a particular ship is a sailboat, the user may want to know the number of sails. For other kinds of ships, the user may want to know different attributes—for powerboats, the horsepower; for yachts, the number of people accommodated; and for dinghies, the number of seats.

It would be a wasteful design to have number of sails, horsepower, number of people accommodated, and number of seats all as attributes of the ship object. With such a design, no instance of a ship would have a value for all four of these attributes, because no ship can be a sailboat and a powerboat and a yacht and a dinghy. So, for most ships, the value of three of these attributes would be null.

Figure 2.2 shows a design for ship object classes using an inheritance structure. Sailboats, yachts, powerboats, and dinghies all inherit the attributes: name, owner, ownerPhone, and ownerAddress, plus the services assignShip and billOwner. The sailboat object class extends the ship definition by adding numberofSails. Powerboat adds horsepower; yacht adds numberSleeps; and dinghy adds numberSeats.

The most powerful aspect of the inheritance concept is illustrated by the fact that, if changes are made to the Ship definition, those changes are automatically inherited by the Sailboat, Power-

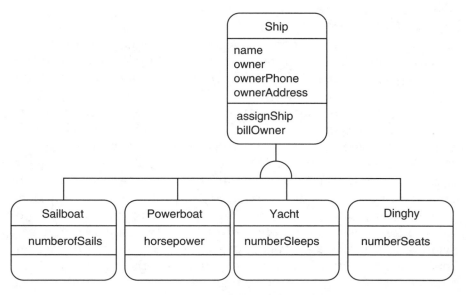

Figure 2.2: An inheritance structure

boat, Yacht, and Dinghy object classes. As with encapsulation, inheritance has powerful implications for software maintenance, reuse, and rapid prototyping. Because inheritance combines extensibility with ease of modification, it makes maintenance, reuse, and rapid prototyping easier, faster, and more fun. For rapid prototyping in particular, a library of reusable object classes may be simply extended when they almost, but don't quite, fit needs, accelerating development and giving the prototyper the confidence of an established base.

Control by Message

One of the most confusing concepts for programmers who are not accustomed to object-oriented development is the fact that software objects are controlled by *messages*. The closest thing to a message in procedural programming languages is a subroutine call. But, to think of services issuing messages as being equivalent to programs issuing subroutine calls is actually misleading, because the subroutine concept is hierarchical and object-oriented software is not.

Hierarchical software is created by writing a driver program, or executive, that makes calls to subroutines; the driver program is in charge. The program is called *interactive* if the user gets to do something once in a while (such as select from a menu) in response to a system prompt. Many programmers are comfortable with the hierarchical approach because it puts them in charge of what will happen through program control.

In contrast, message driven software is passive. The programmer writes many small message handlers (typically much smaller than an average program) that wait patiently for their message to arrive. A message handler begins with a one-line statement commanding itself to trap an occurrence of an incoming message. A common syntax for this statement in advanced OO prototyping environments is of the form, "on <message>." The typical object-oriented software application consists of a large host of message handler scripts, each waiting for its message. This approach makes procedural programmers uncomfortable, because it is difficult for them to predict what will happen during execution, much less be in control of a procedural sequence of events.

If programs written by programmers do not control message driven software, what does? The answer is, events. Object-oriented software must be written so that events trigger the issuing messages. Examples of events are:

- The user clicks a mouse button
- The user tabs into or out of a field
- A new record (object instance) is created
- An object instance different from the currently active object is accessed
- An object class different from the currently active class is accessed
- The specified threshold value of a specified object attribute is exceeded for a specific object instance

Many events, such as the click of a mouse button, are trapped automatically in many object-oriented graphic user interface (GUI) development environments, where use of a mouse is assumed. Thus, the programmer in such an environment does not need to write a low-level software routine to check for an occurrence of a mouse button being clicked. Instead, the programmer can simply write a service that begins with a command like "on mouseup." Such a service will be automatically activated when the mouse button is clicked.

Other events, such as the occurrence of an attribute's threshold value being exceeded, must be detected by a service written by the programmer; the same service would then produce an appropriate message. For example, if one of the attributes of a reactorReading object class is reactorTemp, then a monitorTemp service might have some code in it similar to:

```
while <there are more reactorReadings>
   get <next reactorReading>
      if reactorTemp > 1200
         shutDown
      else . . .
```

The shutDown service would begin with a line such as, "on shutDown." The issuing of the shutdown message by the monitor-Temp service would cause the shutdownReactor service to be activated.

Another example of message generation upon exceeding a threshold would be an Account object class that contained a checkBalance service and a dunCustomer service. The checkBalance service would look at Account attributes such as balanceOwed and dueDate and make a determination as to whether to generate a threatening form letter about the overdue balance. If the decision was yes for a particular Account object instance, the checkBalance service could simply issue the message "dunCustomer" and the dunCustomer service could trap this message by starting with the line "on dunCustomer."

The Many Forms of Polymorphism

The literal meaning of *polymorphism* is the ability to take many forms. In object-oriented software engineering, polymorphism means that objects can interpret messages in their own ways, each using a different method (we say *service*) to accomplish the directive of the message. Objects can send messages to each other without the sending object having to know anything about how the message will be interpreted or the receiving object having to know anything about what was required to generate the message.

The benefit of such polymorphism is that, when object classes are reused, all that need be adjusted is the message trap. If a service that trapped the message "activate" with the line "on activate" is moved to an environment where the same behavior is expected in response to the message "startUp," then "on activate" can simply be modified to "on startUp" and the rest of the service need not be altered. Polymorphism, along with encapsulation, enables object-oriented software development to move away from a hierarchical view of application systems, where all components are tightly coupled to many of the other components, toward a view where object classes are relatively autonomous and require little knowledge of other object classes' data structures or behaviors.

Object-Oriented Analysis

There are currently several object-oriented analysis (OOA) approaches in widespread use. Almost any of the OOA methods providing an object class diagram that models both attributes and services is sufficient, but rapid prototyping works better with simple abbreviated approaches that lend themselves well to concurrency and iteration based on partial preliminary requirements specifications. Some good recommended reading is provided at the end of this chapter. OOA specification methods that demand elaborate implementation details prior to any development will make evolving specifications concurrently with the prototype unneccessarily difficult.

We provide an overview of OOA in Chapter 3, but not very much detail. The reader who wants to study OOA in depth is encouraged to read one of the texts referenced on this subject. We do, however, intend our book to provide enough information to get you well started in developing fast, simple, OOA specifications for a rapid prototype.

Object-Oriented Design

There are also several competing philosophies for object-oriented design (OOD), and again, we opt for the simplest. OOD has been around longer than OOA; this created a unique problem before OOA arrived on the scene. In the mid-1980s, when OOD approaches such as Booch[1] were becoming increasingly popular, structured analysis was still the standard for requirements definition—good OOA alternatives did not exist. This meant that people who wanted to perform object-oriented programming often began with structured analysis for requirements modeling and then attempted to convert dataflow diagrams to Booch diagrams as the design phase of the project began.

When good OOA approaches began to arrive on the scene (late 1980s and early 1990s), there was still not a workable way to transition from the new models to the OOD diagrams of existing OOD methodologies. Later, most of the authors of the new OOA approaches evolved their own OOD approaches. Many simply recommended producing more of the same kind of models used in OOA, but becoming more oriented toward a specific physical implementation environment. This keeps things simple and, again, is well suited to a rapid prototyping approach where analysis, design, development, and test are concurrent activities.

Object-Oriented Programming

This activity has the acronym OOP and the tool used to perform the activity is referred to as an OOPL, object-oriented programming language. There are three classes of OOPL: the basic and pure OOPL (e.g., Smalltalk), the hybrid OOPL (e.g., C++), and the OOPL that is part of a comprehensive object-oriented development environment (e.g., Gain Momentum's GEL™). We prefer the latter class of tool for rapid prototyping.

A GRAPHICAL DEFINITION OF OBJECT-ORIENTED RAPID PROTOTYPING

A model of the object-oriented rapid prototyping process is depicted in Figure 2.3. At this point we will not discuss the details of this model, but rather use it to illustrate that specification development is integrated into the process, and that the procedure encompasses all development phases. The details of the process will be covered in Chapter 6, Development; Chapter 7, Refinement; and Chapter 8, Evolution. Figure 2.3 shows that, for the object-oriented rapid prototyping process:

- Prototype development is based on rapidly developed OO specifications
- Prototype development is object-oriented, consisting of the creation of object classes with encapsulated services
- Prototype iteration repetitively modifies, extends, and refines both the specifications and the existing object classes
- The combination of specifications and existing object data structures, services, and controls becomes the requirements baseline upon user approval of the prototype
- A user-approved prototype can be leveraged into full-scale operational mode by performance testing and tuning.

ENDNOTE

1. Booch, Grady, *Object-Oriented Analysis and Design with Applications*, Benjamin Cummings, Redwood City, CA, 1993.

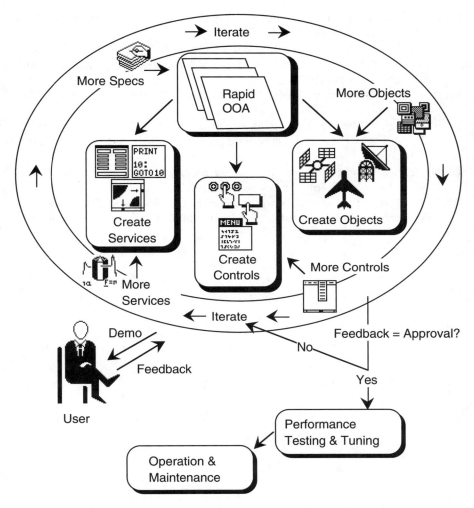

Figure 2.3: The object-oriented rapid prototyping process

RECOMMENDED READINGS

Booch, G., *Object-Oriented Analysis and Design with Applications*, Redwood City, CA: Benjamin Cummings, 1993.

Coad, P., and Yourdon, E., *Object-Oriented Analysis*, New York: Yourdon Press (Prentice-Hall), 1990, 1991.

Coad, P., and Yourdon, E., *Object-Oriented Design*, New York: Yourdon Press (Prentice-Hall), 1991.

Connell, J., and Shafer, L., *Structured Rapid Prototyping*, Englewood Cliffs, NJ: Yourdon Press (Prentice-Hall), 1989.

Jacobson, I., Christerson, Jonsson, and Overgaard, *Object-Oriented Software Engineering: A Use Case Driven Approach*, Wokingham, England: Addison-Wesley, 1992.

Mullen, R., *Rapid Prototyping Object-Oriented Systems*, Reading, MA: Addison Wesley, 1991.

Rumbaugh, J., Blaha, M., Premerlni, W., Eddy, F., and Lorensen, W., *Object-Oriented Modeling and Design*, Englewood Cliffs, NJ: Prentice-Hall, 1991.

Taylor, D. A., *Object-Oriented Information Systems: Planning and Implementation*, New York: John Wiley & Sons, 1992.

Wirff-Brock, R., Wilkerson, B., and Wiener, L., *Designing Object-Oriented Software*, Englewood Cliffs, NJ: Prentice-Hall, 1990.

3
Objects

Various writers have noted, and we have experienced, the fact that identifying the set of required object classes for a new application is difficult. Primarily, prespecification has always been difficult, and new, object-oriented paradigms for systems specification do not provide the silver bullet that eliminates requirements uncertainty. Rapid prototyping can greatly reduce requirements uncertainty, while object-oriented analysis and design provide an improved paradigm for the concurrent development of requirements and design specifications.

Evolving the analysis and design specifications, using object-oriented techniques simultaneously with prototype development and refinement, avoids the following problems:

- *Losing track of the overall application architecture.* When the prototype attains a size of over 30 object classes and over 100 services (still a fairly small system), it becomes difficult to keep track of all the system components without a specification; the scope of understanding will be at the level of one or two object classes and a handful of services at a time.

- *Losing track of versions and contents of prototype modules that have been approved by the user.* Configuration management (which things the user currently approves and what combination of which things is the latest version of the application) will become nearly impossible unless the specifications are kept up to date during prototype iterations.

- *System documentation inaccurately representing the final software system.* Such documentation is worse than useless—it can be dangerously misleading.

Building and delivering a high quality, neatly organized, clearly documented system requires a carefully architected prototype. By starting small and growing the prototype over time, incremental specifications become primarily additions to the specification, rather than modifications to the components of the previous specification. This book provides an approach to modeling the requirements and design of rapidly evolving prototypes using simple object-oriented graphic representations.

Several good methods for object-oriented analysis and design provide usable graphic notations. We recommend in particular: Coad and Yourdon,[1,2] Booch,[3] Jacobson,[4] or Rumbaugh.[5] Ed Yourdon's excellent text, *Object-Oriented System Design*,[6] and Ian Graham's *Object-Oriented Methods*,[7] both do a good job of explaining the equivalences between these and other methods. Our notational style draws on elements of all these, and simplifies so that iterations of the static models can be as rapid as iterations of the prototype. If you already know one of the above referenced notations, you do not have to learn ours. Use any of the above notations for the models, but keep it simple.

IDENTIFYING OBJECTS FOR PROTOTYPING

Some specification-oriented analysts go to the early user interviews and ask for a list of all objects of interest to the users, but that is not exactly the rapid prototyper's approach. Other specification-oriented analysts ask users to prepare a written statement of requirements and then study that document, looking for potential objects. Some combination of these two techniques will probably produce useful results, but the rapid prototyper does not rely on either of them to produce a complete, correct, and exact list of required application object classes. The object-oriented rapid prototyper should look for a small, intentionally incomplete set of initial object classes that can be developed in software and presented to users as an interesting starting point for experimental requirements discovery.

The subset of preliminary object classes for the initial prototype development can be very small. For example, an application system that ultimately consists of 300 object classes might appropriately begin with a prototype consisting of an early version of only 10 object classes. These would be the object classes that both developer and user identify with certainty as part of the real requirements space. If 10 more object classes were added in each prototype iteration, there would be 29 iterations to user approval of the prototype—a reasonable number of iterations for a three- to-six month requirements definition activity with a two-person prototyping team. There is no harm in leaving 290 object classes out of the first version of the prototype. On the other hand, a lot of wasted effort can result from including 290 incorrect object classes in the first version, requiring a lot of unproductive and avoidable rework.

Discussing Objects with Requirements Commissioners

The term *user* has been defined to mean a person who commissions a developer to implement his or her requirements in software. This is not always a person who sits at the keyboard, operating the system. In fact, it is often the case that the total requirements commissioning community will include many people who will not be direct operators of the system. Anyone for whom the system performs services is a stakeholder in the product, is in some sense a user of the system, and will be referred to as a *requirements commissioner*.

It is no surprise that the best way to get started in identifying objects is to go out and talk to requirements commissioners. What questions should be asked? Requirements commissioners do not necessarily think naturally of their problem space in terms of objects. They may need to be led to this viewpoint through talk of the things that are part of their work environment.

Many requirements commissioners, during an interview, want to immediately leap into a discussion of what data the system must be capable of producing in terms of displays, reports, database updates, file maintenance, and device control. Don't fight this tendency. The requirements interview is a place to learn about the user's requirements, not for the user to learn about object-oriented analysis. Ask the user to name the people, databases, files, and devices that will receive output data.

If the talk turns to reports, use this opportunity to find out what are the components (data elements) of the reports. Typically, users speak in terms of collections of ouput data; these collections must be separated into their primitive data component parts. Take notes—all of this information will be useful during initial OOA and prototype development.

Try to get the users to relax about requirements completeness. Let them know that it will be perfectly fine if they forget to mention some required outputs. Tell them the list of required outputs is preferably limited, initially, to only those most certainly required. Explain the preference of aiming for a correct model over a complete one for the initial prototype. Sell them on the fact that rapid prototyping means that other requirements can be easily added as the project proceeds.

Next, discuss the fact that the system will need to acquire information from external sources in order to produce the required outputs. Ask the users where data can be obtained that might be useful as the raw material from which outputs will be manufactured. What are the components of this data? What people, databases, files, and devices can be used as sources of input to the prototype?

Again, the users do not need to be certain that the list of inputs is complete or correct. It is not even the users' problem to determine whether any system will be able to feasibly convert the suggested inputs into the required outputs. The feasibility of the data transformation processing will be tested by prototyping.

Believe it or not, all of the information needed to derive a set of preliminary object classes for an object-oriented analysis suitable for prototype development has probably been collected at this point. Look at the components of the input data. Try to organize groups of components into collections that consist of attributes of a thing to which the user's thoughts and/or actions might naturally be directed. Name that thing, and a prototype object class has been named. Repeat this process for collections of components of required outputs, and the result will be object classes defined as artifacts needed to represent required output or input data. Jacobson's concept of *use cases*[4] is useful in helping to define object classes from the user requirements point of view. Develop scenarios of how users will employ object classes to support performance of specific job duties.

After some potential object classes have been identified, challenge their goodness. The following are guidelines for identifying good object classes:

- A good object class will have multiple instances, each of which will be uniquely identifiable

- A good object class is atomic, it is not compound—it cannot be divided into two or more distinct object classes
- A good object class has multiple attributes that need to be remembered by the application
- No instance of an object class should have any attributes that have a value of "blank," "null," or "n/a"
- A good object class will require services (functions—at least for creation, modification, and deletion)
- Some examples of good types of object classes are external systems, devices, events, document components, persons in roles, procedures, sites, and organizational units

The following is an example of object identification. Suppose a user suggests that some of the information for input to the prototype of a departmental information system is available from the human resources database (HRDB), an external system maintained by the human resources department. The data components of interest in the HRDB are employee ID, name, organization code, skill code, job title, and salary. This collection of attributes suggests an employee object class.

The following is an example of object identification for a real-time system. The system needs to acquire data in real time regarding wind velocity. The components of this data are sensor ID, time, and velocity reading. These attributes suggest a sensor reading object class.

Are these good objects? They are uniquely identifiable (by employee and sensor ID). They are single, indivisible objects with multiple attributes. It does not appear that any of these attributes will ever be blank for any object instance (a person or sensor data point). Both examples of object classes will need services to add, modify, and delete instances. They are simple examples, but adhere to the guidelines for good object classes.

Specifying the Attributes of Objects

Attributes are the information about an object that users are interested in knowing. When objects are identified from collections of external interface components, as above, the attributes are also known. Figure 3.1 shows a graphical representation for the em-

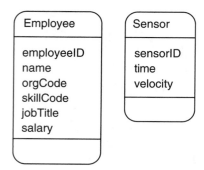

Figure 3.1: Graphic representation of employee and sensor objects

ployee and sensor object classes. The object class name is in the top of the box and the attributes of the object class are listed between the lines within the box.

There is one more step before the object is well defined and well attributed. Challenge each attribute for goodness. The following are guidelines for identifying good attributes:

- A good attribute is a natural part of the description of its object class and is not part of the description of some other object
- The user will have a need to know the value of the attribute for at least some object instances
- A good attribute is atomic, it is not compound—it cannot be divided into two or more distinct attributes
- A good attribute has only one value per object instance—it is not a vector or a list of values
- A good attribute will have a value for every object instance— it will never be "blank," or "null," or "n/a"
- A good attribute cannot be computed from the value of other attributes—it is not a stored computation.

When these guidelines are applied, it is often found that some of the attributes initially associated with particular objects should be removed from their definition because of violation of one or more goodness principles. What should be done with them, if they truly represent information of interest to the user? A new object class can be defined and the exiled attributes can be re-encapsulated within its definition. In the case of compound attributes, they can be divided, producing new attributes to simply add to the original object definition. In the case of stored computations, a service that performs the computation can be encapsulated in the object class.

Imagining the Behavior of Objects and Specifying Services

Object class models provide a prototype blueprint. The prototype must do something for the users. Part of the definition of an object is its behavior—a good object does things. To the Smalltalk programmer, an observable behavior of an object is a *method*. In C++ methods are called *member functions*. Here, we use the Coad/Yourdon term *service*.

Services are encapsulated as part of each object's definition. Minimally, each object class contains services to create, modify, and delete instances of itself. Many application objects will also contain services to perform calculations, provide monitoring and reporting, and provide mechanisms for system navigation and control. Figure 3.2 shows a graphical representation of the employee and sensor objects with specification of encapsulated services. Since create, modify, and delete services are required for every object, they may be assumed and need not be specified in the graphic representation.

How does one know what services to specify and build for the initial prototype? The key is to avoid overspecification. A suggestion of a system, to give the user something interesting to evaluate, something that will stimulate the discovery of further requirements, is all that need be provided. A good way to start is to specify the services needed to capture the inputs from, and produce the outputs to, the external sources and destinations identified in the initial user inter-

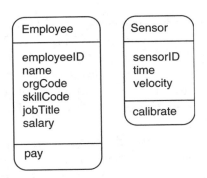

Figure 3.2: Employee and sensor objects with services

views. Each of these initial services will eventually require a definition, but for now, service specifications need not be completed. The initial prototype must be evolved and refined to user approval before assurance that the requirements of services are known.

IDENTIFYING POTENTIAL INHERITANCE STRUCTURES

Once object classes have been identified, specified, and represented graphically, they should be connected on the OOA model to show relationships with instances of other objects. First, let's consider inheritance structure, the very heart of object-oriented software engineering. Whenever an inheritance structure can be identified and specified, a great deal of rework will be saved in the future—a big bonus for iterative prototyping. Changes made at high levels within an object model's inheritance structure will be automatically inherited by the children (subclasses) of the modified parent object classes.

Many inheritance structures can be identified by application of the preceding guidelines for defining good object classes and attributes. If, for example, a collection of object instances have a subset of attributes whose values, for those instances, are "blank," "null," or "n/a," then that collection might be a derived class of the parent object class. In this case, a new object class should be created with a connection to the base object class indicating that the derived class of object "is a kind of" base class object. Many "is a kind of" connections exist between objects in the real world: An automobile is a kind of vehicle; a manager is a kind of employee; a wind velocity sensor is a kind of sensor.

The attributes and services applicable to all derived object classes need be named only once within the graphical representation of the base class object. The derived object classes are all connected to the base object class with "is a kind of" connectors. The derived object classes contain attributes and services that are unique to them—no other derived object classes of that base object class have the same attributes or can provide those same services. However, derived object classes automatically contain all attributes and services specified for their base object class through inheritance. See Figure 3.3 for a graphical representation of an inheritance structure.

Another type of parent-child relationship between objects is the whole-part structure. Instead of an "is a kind of" relationship be-

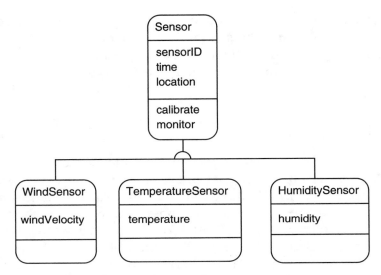

Figure 3.3: An inheritance structure for kinds of sensors

tween the objects there is an "is part of" relationship. The conventional "one to many" types of notational conventions, as described below, adequately define this type of relationship—it is not an inheritance structure.

DETERMINING THE NATURE OF RELATIONSHIPS BETWEEN OBJECTS

All of the objects within an application system are related to some of the other objects in the system. An OOA model shows these relationships as connecting lines. Each object class in an object-oriented requirements specification should be connected to at least one other object class. Further, there should be no disconnected clumps of object classes. A disconnected object class probably belongs in another application system. A disconnected clump of object classes *is* another application system. This is generally true, but exceptions exist for every rule.

If an object class A is related to object class B, then particular instances of object class A will have natural connections with one or more instances of object class B. For example, if object class A is a department and object class B is an employee, then a particular department instance will be connected to particular employee instances for employees who are members of that department.

There are essentially three different types of relationship connections between instances of related object classes:

- one-to-one
- one-to-many
- many-to-many

One-to-one means that for each instance of object class A, there is a related instance of object class B. *One-to-many* means that for each instance of object class A, there can be many related instances of object class B. *Many-to-many* means that object classes A and B both have one to many relationships with each other. In other words, for each instance of object class A, there will be multiple related Bs; but also, for each instance of object class B, there will be multiple related As.

The nature of the many-to-many relationship is inherently unstable and is not change resilient. Its existence should be eliminated from OOA models before proceeding with prototyping. As an example, suppose that a large software company has defined *technical sales support representatives* as one object class and *accounts* as a related object class in a marketing support information system. If most tech reps support multiple accounts, but large accounts are frequently supported by multiple tech reps, then this will be a many-to-many object class relationship.

The reason for identifying relationship connections in the first place is that requirements for critical attributes (to support the specified relationships) will be revealed. For example, is department number a critical attribute of an employee object class? What if the users say they never need to know an employee's department number? There still might be a requirement for a department number attribute in the employee object class if there is a need to support a relationship between departments and employees. The employees who are members of department 13 will be identified as those instances of the employee object class that have 13 as the value of their department number attribute. Perhaps the user wants to know the employee's skill code and skill code has been made an attribute of department rather than employee because it will require less maintenance that way. Modeling these data requirements issues reminds the prototypers to construct their object classes so that they will function correctly during prototype development.

In the case of the many-to-many accounts with tech reps relationship example, how can this relationship be supported with attributes? Will you create multiple employee identification attributes in the account object class? Will you also create multiple account number attributes in the tech rep object class? How many accounts will be the maximum any tech rep will ever be assigned? How many tech reps will be the maximum number ever assigned to one account? Due to the inherent instability in this relationship and the many difficult questions that must be answered, the many to many relationship can and should be simplified. It may be restructured as one-to-many relationships between three related object classes—the two object classes of primary interest and an associative object class. In the marketing information system example this associative object class might be called the TechRep Account Assignment. Such an object class need have only two attributes: account number and tech rep employee number.

Notational Conventions

The literature is full of notational conventions for modeling relationship types in an entity-relationship diagram. Arrowheads, circles, crow's feet, and letters are used to represent the concept *many*. Preferences for a particular notational convention are based on feelings about ease of drawing and clarity of the visual representation. We will use the circles convention throughout this book. In actual practice, your notational convention may be forced on you by your selection of a CASE tool, and that's fine—don't worry about it.

Specifying Point of View

What is the nature of the relationship between aircraft and ground control stations in a real-time aircraft control system? It depends on whether the majority of the objects and encapsulated services of your aircraft control system will be hosted in the aircraft or in the ground control station. From the point of view of an aircraft, the system will have at least one or possibly many ground control stations. From the point of view of a ground control station, it will be responsible for tracking many aircraft.

It may seem obvious that a department *contains* many employees, but it really depends on the nature of the application being developed. One department to many employees makes sense if you are developing an organizational information system, but what if you

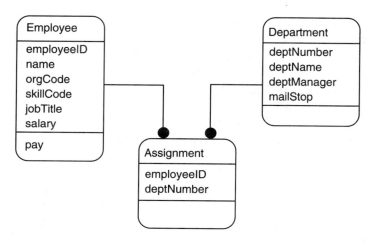

Figure 3.4: Resolving the many-to-many relationship

are developing a personal information system for employees? If your employees are roving internal consultants who work with many departments, then the relationship might be better modeled as one employee to many departments.

When it is impossible (due to specified user requirements) to take only one object's point of view in specifying the cardinality of a relationship between two object classes, then a many to many relationship exists. Figure 3.4 illustrates the many to many resolution using an associative object.

IDENTIFYING SUBJECT AREAS

Subject areas, sometimes called object class collections, are an important complexity-reducing concept of object-oriented analysis. Subjects are particularly important to object-oriented rapid prototypers because of the strong enhancement they provide for reuse. Reused objects, when they are well encapsulated and have been created with tools that made them easy to modify, make excellent *free* components for new prototypes.

Reducing Complexity through Subject Layering

The object-oriented information models of most delivered application systems contain hundreds of object classes. Such models will be very difficult to manage on a computer screen using a CASE tool, because you will only be able to view a small section of the model at any one time. Reviewers and users looking at such models will find them inaccessible and intimidating. There will be difficulties in handing off such models from analysts to designers, designers to programmers, developers to maintenance programmers.

Object-oriented models avoid the change in form and meaning that occurred between structured analysis models, such as dataflow diagrams, and structured design models, such as structure charts. There are object-oriented models of requirements (implementation environment independent) and object-oriented models of design (implementation environment dependent). Both use the same graphic representation and notational conventions. This represents a big improvement in moving from a structured to an object-oriented specification approach.

The structured approaches were, however, very good at managing specification complexity through hierarchical decomposition. This was both good news and bad news for rapid prototypers. The good news was that each page of a hierarchical set of dataflow diagrams could be presented in easily understandable form on standard notebook size paper. The bad news was that modifying the hierarchy of pages during prototype iterations represented unproductive rework and a configuration management nightmare. Other than the context diagram, where system external interfaces were specified, and primitive level diagrams, where the actual system functionality was specified, the middle levels represented only an artificial packaging. Dataflow diagram packaging involved complex rules for balancing, leveling, and partitioning of dataflows and processes, work that had to be modified when system functionality changed during prototyping. CASE tools are helpful in reducing the amount of effort required to do this rework, but do not eliminate it; object-oriented software engineering does.

Subject layering presents a nice compromise between the inaccessibility of large, flat, object-oriented information models and the unwieldly, difficult to modify, long-legged leveling of elaborate dataflow diagram decompositions. A subject area is basically a collection of objects that all relate to the same general area of user interest. Object class models can be reviewed one subject area at a time. An analyst working with a CASE tool can work on one subject area at a time. Small teams of programmers can prototype single subject areas incrementally or concurrently. The printout of a single subject area will probably fit on most desktops. There are not rules (such as seven plus or minus two) for the maximum number of objects allowed in a subject area.

Subject areas do not create balancing and partitioning problems for rapid prototypers. Balancing is not important in object-oriented modeling, because data does not flow, it is encapsulated. Object-oriented services are not partitioned as structured processes were—they are also encapsulated. Encapsulation is good in that it encourages reuse and makes prototype iteration less complicated. Once subject areas have been specified, they tend to be very stable; they do not go away. New object classes can be added to subject layers in prototype iterations, but object classes rarely migrate from one subject to another. This is because subject areas are defined by the semantics of the object classes they contain, an entirely different concept from structured process partitioning.

Reuse at the Subject Level

Whether object classes in common between existing and proposed applications are good strategic targets for reuse depends on the semantics of their particular subject areas. In other words, whether two object classes with the same name are really the same depends on their attributes, services, and connections with other objects. Often a proposed application will have an entire subject area in common with an existing application, in which case all of the existing object classes in that subject area can be reused.

A proposed air traffic control system may not contain the ground control station subject area as part of the target system for reusable components, but both will probably have an aircraft subject area. A proposed motor pool information system and an existing vehicle registration system might have a vehicle subject area in common. An existing harbor information system and a proposed shopping mall security system might have a guard subject area in common. A wind tunnel data acquisition system and a centrifuge control system might have an instrumentation subject area in common.

Use of object-oriented subject layers can resolve some of the troublesome issues we currently experience in attaining high degrees of reuse. Reusable software may be stored in a public repository. Many organizations will elect to migrate objects into existing procedural libraries, gradually phasing out the procedural modules. NASA Ames Research Center has a reusable software library containing a mixture of object-oriented and procedural modules. Difficulties have been reported by programmers trying to reuse some of the procedural software in this repository:

- Many of the large applications must be reused on an all or none basis because of the tight coupling between the non-object-oriented internal components
- Making changes to the software can be tricky because of assumptions about the operating environment built in by the original author and because of the modification difficulties inherent in a procedural language program
- It is difficult to match supply with needs—potential reusers have a hard time finding software that is a good enough fit with their requirements to warrant the difficult rework that will be necessary

If all of the software in the Ames' repository were object-oriented, if object-oriented analysis and design specifications were stored with it, and the specifications were subject layered, all of these difficulties would be mitigated. Tight coupling of components would go away because of designed-in encapsulation—design for reuse. The minimal modifications that would be required to convert the software for reuse in the new environment would be easier because of the greater flexibility of object-oriented languages. Subject layering would make for easier comprehension of the reuse target and provide for the possibility of reusable subject area collections of objects. One of the authors is helping Ames move toward this ideal state by developing standards, writing guidebooks, and providing training and project mentoring that foster and encourage object-oriented analysis, design, programming, and rapid prototyping.

Guidelines for Identifying and Specifying Good Subjects

Reuse at the subject level will be encouraged to the extent that analysts do a good job of subject layering. The following are some suggested criteria for subject layering. The objectives of the criteria are examined one at a time to discover what purposes will be served by modeling to these criteria.

1. Minimize the number of connections between the object classes in the subject being defined and all other object classes in the model (loose coupling).

If object classes are mostly connected to other object classes within the same subject area and rarely connected to object classes in other subject areas, they are contributing to the semantic definition of the subject area. The whole subject area will make more sense to a browser to the extent that this is true. Coupling always reduces reusability. The more tightly coupled an object is to other objects in an application, the more difficult it will be to reuse in a new application. The same applies to subject areas. If a subject area has minimal coupling with other subject areas within a model, there is a good chance that the entire subject area collection of object classes will be easy to reuse in other applications with similar requirements subject matter. Low coupling reduces the ripple effect where modifying one item may cause defects in others. It also makes system specifications easier to understand.

2. Include an object class in a subject area only when it makes a contribution to the semantic definition of the subject area.

It is possible to follow the guideline for minimal coupling between subjects and still have object classes within a subject area that were only included there for packaging convenience (you couldn't figure out where else to put the object class). This will make it difficult to name the subject area—the test for violation of this criterion. If you have trouble naming the subject area, it will have a reduced chance of appearing on a browsing potential reuser's hit list. It will have a reduced chance of being a good fit in any other application subject area.

3. Do not break up an inheritance structure.

Since derived object classes are only *kinds of* their base class objects, the whole inheritance hierarchy is always part of the same semantic definition of a subject area. The only possible reason for separating object classes in an inheritance structure into separate subject areas would be adherence to some arbitrary organizational standard regarding the number of allowable object classes in a subject area. This would be a mistake, particularly if it resulted in the object classes being separately reused in new applications without the benefits that could be derived from the inheritance hierarchy.

4. If a service seems to be forcing an object class to belong to two or more subject areas, break the service up into two or more services and distribute the new services to object classes in the other subject areas.

Breaking up complex services into simpler ones will solve all sorts of problems for you. The reason complex services tend to force object classes to want to belong to multiple subject areas is that they are needing data from multiple object classes in different subject areas. This is in violation of the principle of encapsulation and will result in diminished reuse potential. It will also result in increased maintenance effort, as changes to the model will have a ripple effect involving multiple subject areas.

5. Try to define subject areas that will exist in many other application domains—this is part of designing for reuse.

It need not take extra effort to identify subject areas that will exist in other application domains. It should be second nature to a good designer. Subject areas that make very specific assumptions about a given implementation will tend to become obsolete if the operational life of a system is long enough for requirements to change. This happens to almost all implemented software. Object-oriented software can and will have much longer life expectancy than procedural software due to the extensibility and easy modifiability of object classes. Space Station Freedom software, for instance, may have a life expectancy of thirty years—longer than most software careers.

6. Apply common sense to the tradeoff of complexities among object classes (number of attributes and services), subjects (number of object classes), and models (number of subjects).

It is obvious that modeling an application containing 500 object classes as 20 subject areas, each containing an average of 25 object classes, is superior to modeling those same 500 object classes as two subject areas, each containing 250 object classes. The latter approach produces subject area models that are too complex for easy understandability. It should also be obvious that a model containing 100 subject areas, each with an average of five object classes, is too complex from the point of view of understanding how all the subject areas fit together into a whole application.

Some practitioners desire a numerical guideline such as the old *seven plus or minus two* from structured analysis days. Unfortunately this guideline, although based on sound psychological research regarding limits of human comprehension, is too confining for an object-oriented approach. If we only allowed nine subject areas per application, only nine object classes per subject area, and only nine attributes and/or services encapsulated in each object class, we could only have 81 simple object classes in an application. Many applications have hundreds of object classes with many object classes containing more than nine attributes.

It seems that in object-oriented software engineering, the comprehensibility of a subject area must be traded off for the elimination of a hierarchical functional decomposition that will build ripple effect into a system and make prototype iteration uneccessarily difficult. In other words, you've got to have more that nine object classes in most subject areas, and you've got to have more than nine subject areas in most applications. A better upper limit might be around 30 object classes in each of 30 subject areas, allowing a model of an application to contain 900 object classes. More than 900 object classes might indicate the need to develop two applications, each with its own schedule and budget and its own requirements and design documents.

DESIGNING PROTOTYPE OBJECT CLASSES

So far, this chapter has dealt mostly with object-oriented requirements analysis. It is appropriate to do so because this is a book on rapid prototyping—a requirements discovery technique. However, because a prototyper must develop a prototype as actual operational software, some design is also necessary. The prototype specification cannot be implementation independent, because you will be implementing it immediately.

The design of an object-oriented prototype is no big deal, using object-oriented specification methods. The same models, using the same notational conventions may be used. The following differences exist in an object-oriented design model:

- Objects are created that exist only because of the technology used in the implementation environment
- How the users will control the application components is modeled
- The sequencing of services is modeled
- The actual data structures, as they will be implemented in an actual data management system, are modeled

The object-oriented rapid prototyper will create models of these application components concurrently with the problem domain model. We recommend jumping to implementation-dependent, control-specific models immediately, so that you can begin prototyping within a week or two of project start.

DEVELOPING PROTOTYPE OBJECT CLASSES

This chapter has covered the techniques used in the specification of object classes for object-oriented rapid prototyping. A simple specification of about 10 object classes would be adequate to start development of an initial prototype. Such a very preliminary specification would take about one week, including initial user interviews and peer review of the models, to complete. In another week a prototype based on this specification could be developed and demonstrated to users.

The initial prototype should be built using a very high level OO development environment. The characteristics of such a development environment are discussed in Chapter 4, Tools. One of the important elements of such an environment is a powerful data management system (DMS). The DMS will allow you to create an object as a collection of attributes. Simply create each object shown on the object class model. Other tools within the development environment will allow for rapid creation of encapsulated services. Chapter 5, Development, provides a how-to tutorial on object class and encapsulated service creation.

ENDNOTES

1. Coad, P., and Yourdon, E., *Object-Oriented Analysis*, New York: Yourdon Press (Prentice-Hall), 1990, 1991.

2. Coad, P., and Yourdon, E., *Object-Oriented Design*, New York: Yourdon Press (Prentice-Hall), 1991.

3. Booch, G., *Object-Oriented Analysis and Design with Applications*, Redwood City, CA: Benjamin Cummings, 1993.

4. Jacobson, I., Christerson, Jonsson, and Overgaard, *Object-Oriented Software Engineering: A Use Case Driven Approach*, Wokingham, England: Addison-Wesley, 1992.

5. Rumbaugh, J., Blaha, M., Premerlni, W., Eddy, F., and Lorensen, W., *Object-Oriented Modeling and Design*, Englewood Cliffs, NJ: Prentice-Hall, 1991.

6. Yourdon, E. *Object-Oriented System Design*, New York: Yourdon Press (Prentice-Hall), 1994.

7. Graham, I., *Object-Oriented Methods*, Wokingham, England: Addison-Wesley, 1994.

4

Tools

The odds of successful implementation of OORP increase when the right tools are used. Before describing the actual techniques involved in developing an object-oriented rapid prototype, we will examine the characteristics of rapid prototyping tools and why they are helpful.

The most commonly available prototyping tool in a popular object-oriented programming language (OOPL) today is C++, a hybrid of the C language. A hybrid OOPL is an extension of a procedural language that supports encapsulation, inheritance, and message passing. These languages are created by extending existing compilers, adding new syntax. Programmers using a hybrid OOPL have an advantage in that they do not have to learn an entirely new syntax (Smalltalk is as different from C as Chinese is from Spanish). In fact, using a C++ compiler, a C programmer can easily write conventional C programs that will compile successfully. Thus, conventional procedural programmers can do nothing different and still claim (falsely) that they are now doing object-oriented programming because they are using an OOPL. This concept is so appealing that hybrid OOPLs appear to be outselling the pure OOPLs by an order of magnitude.

The OOPL that is part of a comprehensive object-oriented development environment might be either pure or hybrid. The differentiator is that it is integrated with a rich set of development tools: a class library, a class browser, standard graphic user interface environment built-ins, perhaps visual programming capability for input screen and report generation, and perhaps even an object-oriented data management system. There are an increasing number of tools in this class, they are ideal for OORP, and the value of their use will be assumed throughout this book.

The following material is not a discussion of whether C++ or Smalltalk is the better object-oriented rapid prototyping language. Neither language is as good as some of the more advanced modern tools developed specifically to support rapid prototyping. Either is adequate, with the right set of objects available in a robust class library, but there are OORP environments that go far beyond the limitations of any single OOPL. These very advanced object-oriented development environments provide the support needed to ensure highly productive rapid prototyping. This chapter describes the characteristics of these types of tool suites and mentions a few specific products to illustrate how to evaluate them.

Prototype development tools should allow for an integrated approach to the prototyping of data structure, behavior, and control requirements. The tools also must allow for the capture and output of live data with which the user is familiar. These tools must be capable of creating software that will be just as easy to modify as the analysis specifications. If not, the prototype iteration process will take too long and the software will become difficult to maintain due to poorly designed patching during iterations. The best prototyping tools will allow a user-approved prototype to evolve into an easy-to-maintain production system.

Today, a good rapid prototyping environment is more than just an OOPL. Developer workstations, servers, object-oriented analysis and design modeling techniques, and CASE tools also have important roles to play. The right tool for development without prototyping is slightly different from the ideal tool for successful OORP. This is not to say that you can't prototype with whatever tools happen to be available, but prototyping results will be much improved if a good tool set is used. It is also often surprising to many that the goodness of the tools is not directly correlated with their cost.

ADVANCED OBJECT-ORIENTED DEVELOPMENT ENVIRONMENTS

A software development environment can be thought of as the seat where a developer sits and the things that are available at that seat for use in software creation. In the days before prototyping tools, these things typically consisted of a programming language compiler and a text editor. In the really dark ages, it was a line editor or even punch cards. The programmer communicated to the computer from a dumb terminal.

Today's programmers use intelligent workstations with the computing power of the mainframe computers of the 1960s and 1970s. Entire applications can be developed, integrated, and executed by the developer on the computer at his or her desk. Many advanced prototyping languages are not always compiled, but interpreted at run time on the developer's workstation. This allows for much faster turnaround time during prototype iteration, and, in many cases, compilation to object code is an option when faster execution time is needed. Often these very high level languages allow programs to be written in a small fraction of the time it would take to write a comparable C++ or Smalltalk program because of their simplified syntax. Text editing is now an old-fashioned way to enter a software module into a computer. There are visual programming tools, driven by icons and mouse-controlled point-and-click option selections, commonly known as graphic user interface (GUI) builders. Prototyping tool suites are sometimes part of a commercially available data management system product. Many of these products are even object-oriented (provide implementation support for OO concepts).

OORP development tools should have support for the OO concepts of inheritance, message passing, encapsulation, and polymorphism. Figure 4.1 shows how some current development tools might be evaluated as candidate OORP tools in light of these criteria. This is not a complete list, but rather, a sample of representative tools with which the authors are familiar. Figure 4.1 is in no way intended to endorse or condemn specific products, but rather to illustrate how criteria for OORP development environments can be applied to the evaluation of specific commercial products as a part of project planning. Each of the categories presented should be considered, but of

Product	GUI Development Speed	Modifiable Data Structure	Function Development Speed	Object-Oriented Rating
HyperCard	● ● ● ● ●	● ● ● ● ●	● ● ● ● ●	● ● ●
MetaCard	● ● ● ● ●	● ● ● ● ●	● ● ● ● ●	● ● ●
C++	●		● ● ●	● ● ● ● ●
Forms™	● ● ● ● ●			● ● ●
XVT™	● ● ● ● ●			● ● ● ● ●
NextStep™	● ● ● ● ●	●	● ● ● ●	● ● ● ● ●
ViewCenter™	● ● ● ● ●		● ● ● ●	● ● ● ● ●
Parts™	● ● ● ● ●		● ● ● ●	● ● ● ● ●
PowerBuilder™	● ● ● ● ●	● ● ●	● ● ● ●	● ● ● ●
Protoview™	● ● ● ● ●		● ● ● ●	● ● ● ● ●
Gemstone™	● ● ● ●	● ●	● ● ●	● ● ● ● ●
Versant™	● ● ● ●	● ● ● ● ●	● ● ●	● ● ● ● ●
Build™	● ● ● ●	● ● ● ● ●	● ● ● ●	● ● ●
Gain™	● ● ● ● ●	● ● ● ● ●	● ● ● ● ●	● ● ●
Forte™	● ● ● ● ●	● ● ● ● ●	● ● ● ● ●	● ● ● ● ●

Figure 4.1: Examples of rapid prototyping development tools

course, more categories may be added to this minimum set for a finer degree of environment-specific ratings. There are many other fine automated tools on the market. McCABE TOOLS (MT™), Persistence™, ENFIN™ from Easel, ART∗Enterprise™, Object Management Workbench™, and Kappa® from IntelliCorp, Paradigm Plus™ from ProtoSoft, Project Technology (PT™), Object Team™ from Cadre, Select OMT™, SynchroWorks® from Oberon Software, and SES/objectbench™ from SES, Inc. to name a few. Evaluations based on hands-on product testing within a specific environment are recommended.

There are tradeoffs to be considered with any tool. Relational database management systems, although not originally designed to be object-oriented (inheritance is usually not supported), have proven very effective as rapid prototyping tools. Other environments, such as MetaCard™ and HyperCard,™ are quasi-object-oriented (do not fully support all object-oriented concepts). Languages, such as C++, have full support for object-oriented concepts, but are perhaps not the best rapid prototyping tools because many programmers using C++ have a tendency to produce software that is more complex and thus more difficult to modify than scripts written in a higher level language such as HyperCard's Hyper-Talk™ or PowerBuilder's™ PowerScript™. One of the most critical challenges of object-oriented rapid prototyping is deciding how to make decisions about these tradeoffs when selecting rapid prototyping tools.

Object-Oriented Data Management Systems

Is a commercial data management system (DMS) needed for rapid prototyping? Does it have to provide direct support for OO principles? Developing an object class in a prototype consists of implementing three aspects of the object: its *attributes*, its behavior, and how its behavior is controlled. The attributes of an object class are a set of data elements that comprise the type of information about an object instance in which users are interested. Therefore, defining the data requirements of object classes is an activity critical to OORP.

Software engineers who rely solely on a programming language for software development are stuck with implementing storage of persistent object class instances as file structures within programs. The result is the re-creation of a data management system with each new application. Also, the external files referenced by such programs are independent of the inheritance structure defined by the programs and their data structures must be separately maintained.

Much functionality is available effort-free with a commercial data management system. It is easy to add, modify, and delete object classes, attributes, and object relationships when requirements change during prototype iterations. The object-oriented analysis models described in Chapter 3 can be implemented within a very short period of time (sometimes, literally within moments), using high-level DMS object class creation tools. These persistent object classes will be easily modifiable. Typically, the most extreme modification effort will require text editing a one line object creation statement. In some environments the method for persistent object class creation and modification is entirely visually declarative, using mouse point-and-click techniques.

In commercial DMS products, the tools for implementing object behavior as services are almost always available in the form of an integrated, very high level, scripting language. With the best of these products, object behavior control mechanisms are created using the product's visual programming techniques to declaratively implement menu picks, buttons, and event handlers that will be used to invoke specified services.

Do data management systems for object-oriented rapid prototyping have to be object-oriented? OORP can certainly be performed without an OODMS, but to have one is better. Productivity is leveraged when the inheritance structures modeled in OOA diagrams can be implemented using the OODMS. Services and attributes that are encapsulated in objects created with the OODMS will then be easily reusable. OODMS-created objects exhibiting polymorphism provide additional reuse potential.

Required Features in a Development Tool Suite

The following issues should be considered in selecting tools for an object-oriented rapid prototyping environment:

- Can the data structures of object classes be easily created and modified?
- Can new services be created as rapidly as they can be specified?
- Can services be modified during prototype iterations as rapidly as the corresponding OOA and OOD specifications are modified?
- Can the prototype application control mechanisms be easily created and modified?
- Does the prototype environment have external interface capabilities such that it will be interoperable with software and data structures created outside its boundaries?
- Does the prototype environment support inheritance, encapsulation, message handling, and polymorphism?

Remember that:

- Adding, modifying, and deleting attributes of the object data structures should be no more difficult than text editing an enumerated list of attributes.
- Declarative languages for service development are generally more productive than procedural languages, and compiling should be an option, not a requirement.

- Visual (point-and-click, drag-and-drop) programming should be supported.
- Application control should be provided by visual programming and/or high-level language declaration of pull-down, pop-up menus; clickable buttons; and time/sequence-dependent event handlers.
- An external interface should allow the prototyper to call lower-level language modules from a high-level prototype module, e.g., a visually programmed clickable button that can invoke a C or C++ program.
- At least some of the tools in the rapid prototyping environment should support object-oriented concepts directly (rather than through programming conventions).

OORP Workstations

Some workstations are better at supporting object-oriented development than others. The best object-oriented workstations (OOWs) are typically high-resolution graphic workstations running an operating system that is overlaid with a graphic user interface (GUI). They support windowing, scroll bars, animation, mousing, icons, and pull-down or pop-up menuing. In many cases, these GUI features are graphic objects defined by the object-oriented language used to write the operating system environment for the OOW. The Macintosh™, for instance, has a large library of C++ objects, known as MacApp™, as part of its standard programming environment for third-party applications. The MacApp objects make calls to firmware embedded in the Macintosh to provide uniformly standard windows, menus, and so on across thousands of commercial software applications.

Both users and developers typically have strong individual hardware preferences. But, preferences aside, the choice of a graphic OOW running MicroSoft Windows™, Unix™ with X Windows™ and Motif™, or the Macintosh OS is a smart choice for the object-oriented rapid prototyper. These machines are likely to support good object-oriented rapid prototyping tools. They can be stand-alone development environments where the perhaps sluggish performance of an early prototype will not bother anyone. They can support a host of related tools valuable to a software developer such as CASE, word processing, drawing, and desktop publishing.

OBJECT-ORIENTED RAPID ANALYSIS AND DESIGN TECHNIQUES

The best OORP approach is concurrent development and refinement of object-oriented specifications with a rapid prototype during iterations. Good tools are essential to prototype software development, and good modeling approaches are essential to specification development. Considerations in selecting modeling approaches to include in an OORP specification tool suite should be

- Are the models graphics-based?
- Are the methods published?
- Are the modeling methods rigorously nonambiguous?
- Is there a way to model the structure and type of application data?
- Is there a way to model the user interface and application control?
- Is there a way to model application behavior?
- Do the methods provide a means for specifying encapsulation, inheritance, message handling, and polymorphism?
- Are there robust CASE tools available to support these approaches?
- Can a useful set of integrated graphics-based models of data, control, and behavior be prepared with no more than 40 hours effort?
- Will changes to the graphic models be no more difficult than changes to the prototype?

Graphics-based models provide clarity of meaning with less effort on the part of the developer than do narrative specifications. If the methods for preparing such models are widely published and widely read, communications among developers, between developers and management, and between consultants and/or subcontractors and project managers will be improved. Project critical success factors, such as selection of CASE tools and training, will be more easily met. Since requirements come in three dimensions—data, control, and behavior—a good specification tool suite will provide integrated models for each dimension. An object-oriented specification method provides a means for graphically showing services encapsulated with which data attributes in object classes. Inheritance hierarchies are modeled as shown in Chapter 2. Finally, to provide an understanding of message handling and polymorphism, a model showing services provided by each object class on receipt of specified messages is needed.

Prototyping should be a *rapid* process utilizing a set of core specifications. The specification process should not take longer than the software development process. If specifications cannot also be derived rapidly, then the project may not be a viable OORP candidate. The preliminary specifications cannot consume several months without destroying the rapid prototyping momentum. A good initial prototype, built with the right tools, will only take about 40 hours to develop; why should its specifications take any longer? If required changes to the specifications resulting from a one-hour prototype demonstration consume several weeks of effort, it is another indication that the approach is not appropriate for rapid prototyping. The right methods will allow such changes to be made to the prototype specifications in about 8 to 16 hours.

Some currently published approaches to object-oriented analysis and design are not completely compatible with rapid prototyping. They are either incomplete or require too much detail. The incomplete methods have forgotten to provide support for one or more of the modeling requirements listed above. The more complete methods often have many different types of very detailed models that must be prepared before development can begin, often requiring months of preliminary specification effort. The specification tools described below are based on the methods referenced in Chapter 3, Objects, but they have been simplified to expedite the OORP process.

Source/Sink Diagram

Before prototyping can begin, the object classes to be included in the initial prototype must be defined. In turn, before an object class model can be developed, object class names must be chosen. This is not as easy as it sounds. Where do they come from? Scanning preliminary high-level project documents for occurrence of nouns is a trick often recommended and there is no doubt it will yield lots of potential object class names. The problem is, it will yield too many potential object classes with no guidelines for determining which are the best ones for the initial prototype.

Each of the candidate object classes could be subjected to the five tests of good object classes provided in Chapter 3. The ones failing the tests could then be eliminated. Given that the key operative word is *rapid*, it may be more effective to provide the minimum set required for the initial prototype as determined by your requirements commissioners. What is needed is a model that simply and elegantly captures those initial discussions—a model that can depict the overall mission and boundaries of the system and can be used to derive the other models. This model is called the source/sink diagram.

Begin the source/sink diagram by listing some outputs the system must produce: screens, reports, file updates, device control. Find out which people, files, and devices will receive the output. Ask the user what the components are of the outputs. Determine where input data will come from and what its components are. As with destinations, people, files, and devices are the primary types of possible system externals.

Now you can begin drawing your source/sink diagram. Draw a big box in the center—this represents your application. Draw a bunch of little boxes at the edges. These represent the sources and sinks of your application dataflow to and from external entities: people, files, other applications, and devices. So far this is much like a context dataflow diagram from structured analysis, but the similarity ends there, as the source/sink diagram will not be decomposed to lower level diagrams. Instead, the collection of object classes that will appear on the object class model and in the initial prototype will be added now.

Organize the components of the input and output data into collections that consist of attributes of a thing to which the user's thoughts and/or actions might naturally be directed. What are the names of those things? Put named boxes representing the things into the middle of the big box drawn to represent the system and direct the appropriate dataflows to and from the appropriate object classes. This is a natural way to define object classes as they are essentially data abstractions with associated behavior.

The source/sink diagram is a complete high-level specification of the overall requirements of the initial prototype. It specifies that the identified object classes will contain attributes to capture the connected inputs from specific sources and will provide the services necessary to deliver the connected outputs to specific destinations. Do not bother adding object connections, attribute lists, or services yet; those components will be shown on the object class model, which will be developed next, and will be derived from the source/ sink diagram. Figure 4.2 shows a generic example of a source/sink diagram.

Object Class Model

The form of object class model recommended here graphically depicts objects and their encapsulated attributes and services. It also shows inheritance structures, other types of object connections, and subject layers. Message connections are not depicted because the mechanisms for message handling are depicted in the object control matrix, described in the next section.

The object class model shows objects as constructs that will implement information storage and encapsulated services as characteristics of real world things of interest to the user in the application to be developed. Chapter 3 illustrated the graphical representation of an object as a box with rounded corners and two lines through it. On top of the top line, the object name is specified. Between the two

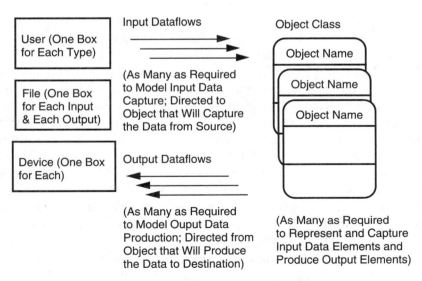

Figure 4.2: Object source/sink diagram graphical notation

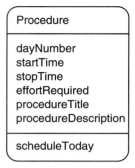

Figure 4.3: Graphic representation of a procedure object

lines, the object's attribute list is specified. Below the bottom line, the list of services to be provided by the object is specified. Figure 4.3 shows a generic graphic representation of a *procedure* object that might be part of a scheduling application.

The object class model also shows connections between objects. These are used to show how certain object classes are derived from other object classes, and therefore will inherit all their attributes and services, and also to show that certain object classes will be allowed to share data. The principle of encapsulation says that an object has everything it needs to perform its services, but this ideal is often compromised in real-world applications in order to create services that meet user requirements.

As illustrated and described in Chapter 3, inheritance connections (showing the hierarchy of object derivation) are indicated by a semicircle connector. Any single object class may have an unlimited number of derived object classes, all strung out on a line connected to the semicircle which is connected to the base class object. Another level of inheritance may be added by deriving new object classes from one or more of the existing derived classes. No limit of inheritance levels is imposed. Some languages, such as C++, support multiple inheritance (an object class can inherit attributes and/or services from multiple base classes). We discourage the use of this feature in early fast prototyping on the grounds that it will create problems in understanding and modifying the prototype. An object class model depicting a lot of multiple inheritance connections will look like a bowl of spaghetti (difficult to tell what is connected to what). Some published C++ guidelines warn against use of multiple inheritance for this reason. The advantages of enhanced reuse and easy maintainability are diminished by use of multiple inheritance.

Chapter 3 covered subject areas: These are an important notational convention on the final object class model, but not on the initial version, which serves as a specification for the initial prototype. The early object class model will not have enough subject areas to make subject layering very interesting. During prototype iteration subject layering will be introduced to control complexity. The idea is to bound easy-to-understand subject areas, which can be worked on and reviewed one at a time. When object classes in the model proliferate to the point of being difficult to remember it may be time for subject layering.

To define a subject area, simply draw a boundary around the object classes to be contained within the proposed subject area. When several subject areas have been defined, different views of the model, except the one currently under development, can be created by collapsing each subject area to a labeled box. Figure 4.4 shows such a collapsed view of real-time wind tunnel operational software.

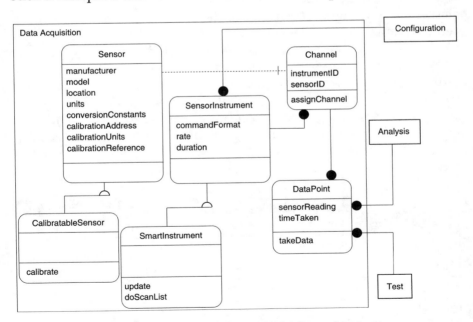

Figure 4.4: Expanded data acquisition subject area

The expanded portion of the model shows the object classes that are involved in acquiring data from wind tunnel sensors.

Object Control Matrix

A question that may occur to the prototype designer after completing the initial source/sink diagram and object class model is, "What will cause these object classes to provide the specified services?" Even annotating the object class model with message connections will not answer this question, because such an annotation cannot possibly describe exactly which message will invoke which service. For those who feel this is a serious problem, the object control matrix is suggested as a solution. This diagram specifies exactly how object class services will be controlled within the prototype.

In an OO application, messages are used to invoke the services of object classes. Whatever mechanism is used to send a particular message, any object can easily be made to trap the message by simply beginning one of the object's services with a one-line message trap such as, "on messageName." An object control matrix is basically a spreadsheet with the rows being all of the application's object classes and the columns being all of the application's messages. Each cell in the matrix specifies what will happen when the object in that row receives the message in that column—perhaps nothing, or perhaps a specified service. The same message can be used to invoke multiple services from multiple objects, in which case the objects could receive the message concurrently and thus could participate in concurrent processing by all executing the invoked services at once. Figure 4.5 shows the appearance of an object control matrix (OCM).

During prototype iteration, users will need to be able to generate every output and execute a service that captures every input on

OBJECTS	MESSAGES			
	Message 1	Message 2	Message 3	Message 4
Object 1	Service 1		Service 5	
Object 2		Service 2	Service 2	Service 2
Object 3		Service 3	Service 6	Service 3
Object 4		Service 4		

Figure 4.5: The object-control matrix

the source/sink diagram. Therefore, it will be necessary to create an OCM model that includes user-generated messages to invoke the services that do these things. Some of these user-generated messages will be artificial, particularly in the case of embedded and autonomous software applications. In such cases the message generators are created only for the purpose of allowing requirements commissioners to exercise critical services in the early versions of the prototype; they do not necessarily become part of the final system.

What can prototypers do if the processing that must happen when an object receives its intended message is quite elaborate? The implication of the object control matrix is that an object can only provide one service in response to each message. This implication is not true, however. An object can provide several services in response to a single message. One way to accomplish this would be to have one of the desired services trap a message from the user or an external event and then issue messages to invoke the other services. These latter messages would then have their own column in the OCM. This is another reason that message annotations on the object class model don't work very well. Here we have an example of an object sending a message to itself.

RAPID PEER REVIEW TECHNIQUES

Don't forget walkthroughs (variations of "reviews" or "inspections"). Less formal and threatening than a management review, more structured and useful than a casual technical discussion, walkthroughs are an important rapid prototyping tool, if you want to make sure that specifications end up accurately documenting the prototype. This book, others, and your own organizational software development standards provide design guidelines. A walkthrough is the best way to ensure that those guidelines are followed in a sensible way.

Inspections and/or walkthroughs save development time rather than increase it by removing defects in analysis and design before they are committed to code (where they will take longer and be more expensive to remove). For this reason, the walkthrough can also play an important role in making rapid prototyping more rapid. To accomplish this objective, a few conventions of rapid walkthroughs must be observed:

- Uncover errors but do not correct them during the walkthrough
- Exclude management of the developer*
- Exclude customers of the developer*
- Exclude anyone who influences the developer's performance evaluation*
- Limit the event to one hour
- Limit the number of participants to no more than six
- Don't use walkthroughs to review software, only specifications
- Classify discussion items as defects, suggestions, and action items
- Don't use walkthroughs to evaluate job performance
- Have a trained coordinator on hand to enforce these conventions

The peer review serves to remove errors before they become defects, an embarrassment at management or customer reviews. If items are classified by the coordinator after no more than five minutes discussion, an amazing amount of specification can be reviewed in one hour by a small efficient team of peers. This describes a rapid walkthrough and it will speed up the prototyping process by efficiently removing mistakes *before* they are prototyped.

A GOOD OBJECT-ORIENTED RAPID PROTOTYPING ENVIRONMENT

The following is an example of an OORP tool suite that is inexpensive (less than US $5,000), easy to acquire, and easy to learn to use. It isn't very powerful, but it is adequate for producing object-oriented rapid prototypes for a small project or throw-away prototypes for large projects. Most people will be able to find an environment similar to this somewhere within their organization, although not always within the software development group:

---

* Don't waste time arguing the merits of these criteria for a quick technical peer review within your organization. Call these events whatever will make them a politically acceptable, true peer review. Managers and customers are welcome to attend as many formal milestone reviews as they care to schedule. Customers are strongly encouraged to attend prototype demonstrations.

- HyperCard
- Macintosh Personal Computer
- Your favorite word processor
- Your favorite drawing program
- This book

For PCs, there are comparable HyperCard compatible (will convert and execute HyperCard applications) products for MS Windows. For Unix Workstations, MetaCard ($500) is totally equivalent to HyperCard and GainMomentum (very powerful, but more expensive) with GEL Script™ will give you HyperCard-like prototyping power and fast multi-user performance against large data stores as well.

HyperCard is a quasi-object-oriented data management system with high-level tools for service development, including visual programming and a scripting language called HyperTalk. HyperTalk scripts are invoked at run time by messages—usually user-generated through devices such as visually programmed mouse-clickable buttons.

HyperCard buttons sit on "cards." Cards also typically contain fields; hence encapsulation and data abstraction. Services are contained in buttons and encapsulated in fields that are attributes of the object represented by the card. A single card is really an instance of an object.

HyperCard allows for the definition of backgrounds to be shared by multiple cards. Background fields and background buttons will appear on every card having the defined background. An individual card within a background can add its own unique buttons and fields, but automatically contains the buttons and fields defined for its background. This is one way HyperCard supports inheritance.

HyperCard applications always consist of one or more "stacks," and the application can be started by double-clicking on the icon of one of the stacks. A stack consists of one or more backgrounds and one or more cards for each background. Multiple stacks can be open at the same time on the user's screen, appearing as resizable windows, and the stacks can be made to communicate with each other through messages. Besides buttons, services can be encapsulated in any HyperCard "object"—fields, cards, backgrounds, stacks—and

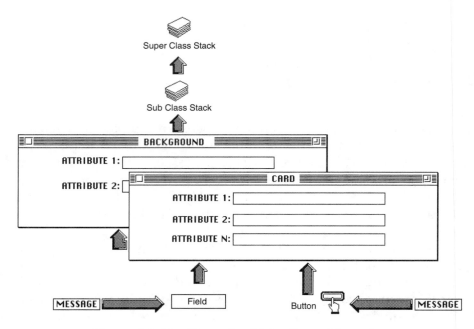

Figure 4.6: The HyperCard inheritance hierarchy

invoked with messages such as "on mouseUp," "on enterField," and "on openCard."

The biggest weakness of HyperCard as an object-oriented development environment is the nonstandard way that it supports inheritance, illustrated in Figure 4.6. This can be corrected by using AppleScript™, which is a true object-oriented high-level scripting language with base and derived classes definable by the developer, instead of HyperTalk, for writing HyperCard services. Multiple stacks can be created and used to instantiate the objects represented in OOA and OOD modeling.

Other advantages of HyperCard are

- Fast creation and modification of objects and services
- Graphics require no coding—just draw with drawing tools
- Word processing services automatically provided
- One can see effects of changes immediately without breaking concentration to compile

All of these advantages are true of the MS Windows and Unix HyperCard-like products as well.

5

Development

This is an important chapter because it provides a how-to tutorial on developing an object-oriented rapid prototype. The tasks that will be required to develop the initial prototype, from planning through preliminary analysis, design and implementation, are described in detail. Development of the initial analysis and design specifications and development of the initial prototype are brief efforts, typically consuming about one week's elapsed time each, one reason this process is called rapid prototyping.

Chapter 4 explained how and why the tools and techniques used for object-oriented rapid prototype development are somewhat different from the tools that might be used in other object-oriented software development projects. No specific prototyping product was advocated, but the use of a *type* of quick-build, object-oriented, prototyping tool was recommended. Building the initial prototype will vary from one vendor's product to another, depending on the syntax and the developer's interface chosen. Nevertheless, the formalized approach to development of the initial prototype may be applied, unchanged, to a number of prototyping tools.

Given the large variety of tools available, it is not possible to provide the specific syntax-related knowledge needed to build a prototype using a particular product. The features of such products that make them easy to use for quick prototype development, and easy to use for making rapid modifications to the prototype, also make such products extremely easy to learn; as a rule, they are simple tools! The learning curve for prototyping tools typically requires less attention than mastering the art of a formalized approach to rapid prototyping. The line between hacking and total prespecification is clearly drawn, separating the two worst evils of software engineering. It is toward this type of awareness that guidance is offered here.

This chapter describes prototype development to the point where it is ready for demonstration to the requirements commissioners for the first time. This development will take from one week to two months on an actual project, depending on size and complexity of the application and project politics. The reason that the initial prototype is ready for demonstration so rapidly is that it is *intentionally* incompletely specified and developed with very advanced quick-build tools. Iterative refinement and evolution of the prototype to a complete, deliverable software application will still take many iterations over many months after this initial demonstration. The refinement process and evolutionary steps are covered in Chapters 6 and 7.

PLANNING AN OORP PROJECT

The first and most critical task of any rapid prototyping project is to develop a written agreement between requirements commissioners and developers, defining goals, approach, scope, tools, responsibilities, deliverables, and schedule for the project. Object-oriented rapid prototyping is different from other approaches to software development. There must be some documented evidence of understanding and agreement on these differences by all parties associated with the project. This written agreement can be called the project plan and should be the first deliverable of an OORP project. Figure 5.1 is an actual example of such a project plan.

RAPID OBJECT-ORIENTED ANALYSIS

It is important to determine prototype components before starting the analysis activity itself. Object-oriented requirements models described in Chapter 4 can be used effectively to specify the initial prototype in a minimal amount of time—say, one or two weeks. The tutorial prototype that follows begins with preliminary interviews with the requirements commissioners. It isn't necessary to be overly cautious or overly thorough about requirements specification at this point—rapid prototyping means that it is okay to be wrong, and incompleteness is actually encouraged. The rapid analysis models produced here will provide object-oriented graphic descriptions of the

Project Plan for Rapid Prototyping of Harbor Information System

Revision Date _____ Revision Number _____

Project Justification: The manager of a yacht club is in need of software to automate boat slip rentals and monitor the security of harbors.

Goal: Provide a computer-based application for rapid retrieval of decision-making information on guards, slips, harbors and ships; personnel management of guards; monitoring harbor security status; and slip rental bookkeeping functions.

Scope of work: Two developers and the harbor manager will comprise the team. The system will be delivered within 3.5 months from the start date.

The tools used to prototype the system will be object source-sink diagrams (OSSD), object-oriented information models (OOIM), object control matrices (OCM), an object-oriented or object-based prototyping tool such as HyperCard on the Macintosh or PowerBuilder on a PC, and a personal computer platform.

User Responsibilities: The harbor manager will participate in the development of the OOSD, OOIM, OCM and will attend each demonstration of a prototyped version of the application, providing timely feedback. She will also provide test data. The harbor manager is responsible for approval of the final product.

Deliverable Product: The product will provide a menu-driven interactive harbor management system in a point-and-click, visual interface environment. A prototype version will be delivered for user approval. The final version will provide data entry and manipulation windows for all objects; information retrieval in the form of harbor reports; services in the form of operations to create new instances of guards, harbors, ships, contracts; scheduling and assignment of guards to harbors; contracting with ship owners to rent harbor slips; and monitoring of the security status of all harbors.

Figure 5.1: Harbor Information System project plan

application's external interfaces, data storage, functionality, and control mechanisms. They will be used to develop the initial object classes with encapsulated attributes and services and to develop the message-generating control mechanisms needed to allow the user to test drive the initial prototype.

The most important model to be produced is the one that shows application data as attributes of an object. This is referred to as the object class model. We recommend, however, that another model, the source/sink diagram, be developed first, graphically depicting the external interfaces for the application. The source/sink diagram was described, in general terms, in Chapter 4. Also, in order to model control of the prototype from the user's point of view, we recommend an additional diagram called the object control matrix, also described in Chapter 4.

The development of these diagrams for an example, called the "Harbor Information System" tutorial, is described in the following paragraphs. If this were a real rapid prototyping project, it would be appropriate to spend no more than two weeks interviewing users, preparing the three diagrams based on information gleaned from the interviews, conducting a peer review of the diagrams, and making necessary refinements prior to beginning prototype development. The total specification for the prototype would occur immediately after agreement on the project plan. It would consist of approximately three pages of graphic, object-oriented diagrams.

Developing the Source/Sink Diagram

Before the object class structures can be modeled, some objects must be identified. In our experience, asking users or requirements commissioners what objects to model does not produce useful results. It is the developer's job to define proposed objects and ask the requirements commissioners if they are reasonable. Below is a suggested approach for quickly defining a set of preliminary proposed objects that will be good enough for the initial prototype.

As described in Chapter 4, begin by asking requirements commissioners to list examples of types of information output the system must be capable of producing: displays, reports, database or file updates, and device control data. Next, ask them to name the type of users, or names of files, databases, or devices to which this data will be delivered. Ask them to think about and suggest the kinds of data that might be available to feed into the application to provide raw materials for producing the required outputs. Determine from which people, files, databases, and devices this data can be obtained.

For a particular application, the identified outputs might include reports needed by management, updates posted to a customer's database, a real-time status display, and automatic signals sent to a device controller. Available inputs for this application might include data entry by the system operators, query results from the customer database, and real-time data readings from sensors. The first diagram of rapid object-oriented analysis, the source/sink diagram, captures the knowledge about these external interfaces and uses it to derive the initial object classes that will populate the initial object class model and the initial prototype. Figure 5.2 is a generic example of a source/sink diagram. The example illustrates how the initial object classes are derived as information repositories that capture incoming data and generate outgoing information. The object classes are identified and named by identifying real-world *thing* the components of the input and/or output dataflows are abstracting.

The following Harbor Information System example illustrates some of the concepts of rapid object-oriented analysis. It is intended to be tutorial only and is not based on any real application system. Examples seem to serve better as tutorials than do real projects, due to inherent complexities of the latter. Real case studies are included in Chapter 9, Experience.

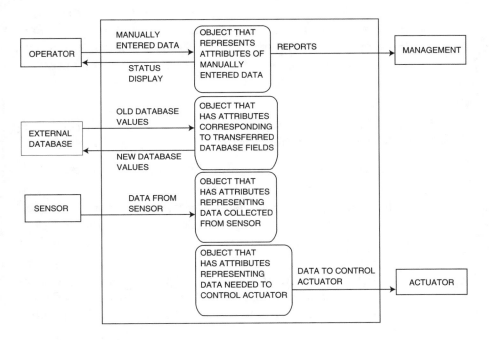

Figure 5.2: Generic object source/sink diagram

Suppose that you are hired as the consultant who will develop the small custom application to be hosted on a personal computer to provide security and slip rental information to the management of a yacht club, as described in the project plan in Fig. 5.1. The hypothetical yacht club spans harbors at multiple sites and maintains a large staff of security guards. The guards patrol the harbor to insure the secure status of boats to the harbor clientele. You will use object-oriented rapid prototyping in order to develop this application.

Your first step is to interview the harbor manager. She tells you that she has four personal requirements from the system:

1. She needs the ability to enter, store, and retrieve information about ship rentals.

2. Periodically, she must be able to pull a report on the percentage of slips rented at each harbor.

3. In her management of the guards, she needs to assign them to patrol duty and she wants the system to be able to produce a duty roster and to issue paychecks on payday.

4. Finally, she wants to monitor the security status of all harbors, in real time, from her office. She feels it is a reasonable request since guards carry devices that transmit an alarm signal when they spot something suspicious at one of the slips.

In addition to her managerial requirements, the harbor manager tells you that the system must provide three other functions:

1. Produce contracts and monthly bills for ship owners.

2. Maintain personnel profiles on guards. Guards are provided, along with their electronic personnel profile, by the Acme Placement Agency. The personnel profile for each new guard should be loaded into the Harbor Information system.

3. Additionally, the hiring of a new guard should automatically generate a purchase order for shoes to Payless Shoes, as free shoes are provided to the club's guards as a fringe benefit.

This is a typically incomplete and ambiguous user's statement of requirements, but it is sufficient to derive the source/sink diagram shown in Figure 5.3. It is obvious that the harbor manager is a very important external interface, providing and receiving much of the system's information. So we provide her with a box outside the system boundary and show her providing new rental information and patrol assignments and receiving the harbor status and the slip-percentage-rented report. From the interview, we also discovered that the system must get guard profiles from the Acme Placement Agency Database and alarm signals from guards' alarm devices. The system must deliver contracts and bills to ship owners, shoe orders to Payless Shoes, and paychecks and duty rosters to guards. All of these requirements are illustrated in Figure 5.3.

The middle of Figure 5.3 is filled with object classes. The analyst determines what these objects are by further inquiry as to the composition of the input and output dataflows. For instance, most of the data elements on a new rental form consist of information we want to know about the ship that will be renting space in our harbor: name of ship, owner's name, owner's telephone number, owner's

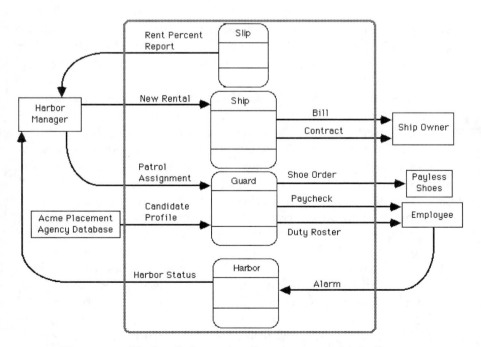

Figure 5.3: Harbor Information System source/sink diagram

telephone address, type of ship, and size of ship. These data elements form an abstraction of a ship object class.

Developing the Object Class Model

The next step in rapid object-oriented analysis is to develop a model of the structure of this initial set of object classes. We can begin by identifying attributes and services for each object class. It is helpful to draw the object classes from the source/sink diagram on a new sheet of paper (or screen). If a computerized drawing tool is being used, simply copy the source/sink diagram, then delete external interfaces and information flows between external interfaces and objects. Assign attributes to the object classes (nouns on the information flows) and determine object instance connection possibilities by role playing ("From the harbor's perspective, many slips are connected").

Object identification by role playing will uncover the usual many to many problems that exist in most applications. For instance, guards are connected to several harbors on their duty roster and harbors are guarded by several guards. This will create a problem in specifying the attributes of such objects. How many harbor attributes should a guard have? How many guard attributes should a harbor have? These are important questions that will need to be answered in order to produce a duty roster.

At first it might seem reasonable to ask the harbor manager to specify the desired number of guards on duty at each harbor at any given time and to specify the maximum number of harbors a guard is to patrol in one duty shift. A better solution is to create a new associative object class, as described in Chapter 3, that resolves this many-to-many problem. This object class, call it "patrol round," would contain guard and harbor identification attributes. These identification attributes provide the link to all other attributes for a given guard or harbor, when and if they are needed. If each instance of "patrol round" had a date, then the collection of instances for a particular guard would constitute all assigned harbors for that date. If start time and end time attributes were also added, this object could perform an encapsulated service to produce a duty roster.

Figure 5.4 shows part of the initial object class model for the Harbor Information System. It shows the guard-to-habor many-to-

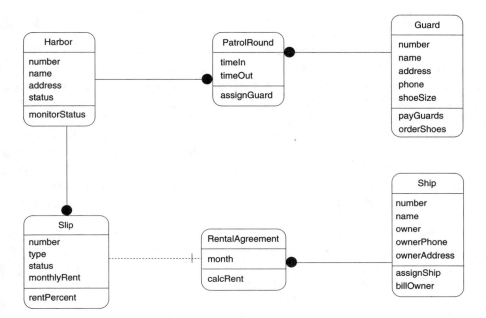

Figure 5.4: Harbor Information System object class model

many connection resolved with the new "patrol round" associative object class. It also shows a many-to-many relationship between slips and ships resolved with the new "rental agreement" associative object class. A ship may rent space in more than one of our harbors at the same time (weekend sailors may choose to have Saturday lunch at one yacht club and Sunday brunch at another). Also, we keep a record, over time, of slip rentals. Often, associative object classes, such as patrol round and rental agreement, are where the more important services of the application will be found.

Figure 5.4 is not complete yet, because there is inheritance in this application that is not yet modeled. The harbor manager tells us that there are many different types of slips and that we charge different rates for each type. Ships are assigned to slips based on type of ship. Ships are classified as one of four types: sailboats, powerboats, yachts, and dinghies. For each type of ship, charges vary according to size within that type. For sailboats, size is determined by number of sails; for powerboats, horsepower; for yachts, number of berths; for dinghies, number of seats. The harbor manager explains that the theory behind this strange algorithm is that it determines the owner's ability to pay better than using the ship's dimension's.

You could add numberofSails, horsepower, numberSleeps, and numberSeats attributes to the ship object class, but then three of these four attributes would be null for any particular ship instance. Null, or not always applicable attributes suggest an opportunity for an inheritance structure. In this case, sailboats, powerboats, yachts, and dinghies are all kinds of ships and should be modeled that way as shown in Figure 5.5. This type of modeling is preferred, because when changes to the data or service requirements are needed (and rapid prototyping iterations always involve many changes), changes made to the base object class will be automatically inherited by the derived object classes.

Inheritance, when used widely throughout an application, will save enormous amounts of rework during prototype iteration, testing, and maintenance phases of the product lifecycle. Inheritance also has reuse benefits. An object class obtained from a software library may be customized by extending the attributes and services in a derived class. Then, if the author of the original object class makes any changes, those changes can be automatically inherited by simply including the new version of the object class in this application (the derived object class will automatically inherit the original author's

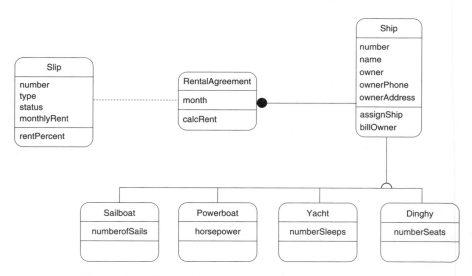

Figure 5.5: Kinds of ships in an inheritance structure

changes). Inheritance also benefits rapid object-oriented analysis specification during prototype iterations. Since the object class model specifies inheritance, changes made during analysis will require fewer changes than in non-OO models.

Modeling Control by Messages Using the OCM

The services specified on the object class model require a method of invocation. In an object-oriented environment, this will happen when the object class in which the service is encapsulated traps its invoking message. The object control matrix (OCM) models how each service is invoked.

Begin by creating a matrix where each row is one of the objects from the object class model. Then, for each object class, list its services in cells across that row. For the Harbor Information System, the rows of the OCM would be:

Harbor   Ship
PatrolRound   Sailboat
Guard   Powerboat
Slip   Yacht
RentalAgreement   Dinghy

There are no services of the derived object classes of ships that cannot be inherited from the Ship object itself, so Sailboat, Powerboat, Yacht, and Dinghy drop out of the matrix. If, for example, the user wants to assign a new Yacht to a Slip, then a message is sent to the Yacht object. Because there is no service associated with Yacht, the message travels up the inheritance hierarchy, is trapped by the assignShip service in the Ship object, and invokes that service.

Once the services of an object have been arranged in cells across its row in the matrix, it must be decided what message the service will trap in order to provide functionality. Some services of multiple object classes might be invokable by the same message. This might be desirable for consistency of the user interface. A "new" message, for instance, might be trapped by services within the Guard (orderShoes), PatrolRound (assignGuard), Ship (assignShip), and RentalAgreement (calcRent) object classes. When this is desired, put the services to be invoked by that single message in the same column as shown in Figure 5.6.

Messages can be generated by:

- user action such as a mouseclick
- a service
- occurrence of a specified time
- threshold violation
- object class access
- object instance access
- attribute access
- data integrity check

Messages must be generated by a service. Message generating services are encapsulated in object classes. In the visual grammar of graphical user interface (GUI) design, a radio button, placed in an interactive window, is a control object. For rapid prototyping, it is not necessary to clutter up your object-oriented information model with low-level design objects such as radio buttons; the object control matrix answers questions about user control of the prototype in a simple fashion at a higher level of abstraction.

Now the rapid object-oriented analysis specification is complete and ready to use to develop a prototype. It consists of three pages of graphic models: the source/sink diagram, the information model, and the control matrix. They show what the purpose of the application is, what information and functionality are required, and how the prototype will be controlled. The Harbor Information System analysis scenario might have gone something like this: The harbor manager is interviewed in the morning, the models are created in the afternoon, and prototyping begins the next morning. This is not analysis paralysis!

	MESSAGES			
OBJECTS	Payday	MonthEnd	New	EndContract
Guard	PayGuards		OrderShoes	
RentalAgrmt		CalcRent	CalcRent	CalcRent
Ship		BillOwner	AssignShip	BillOwner
Slip		RentPrcnt		

Figure 5.6: Harbor Information System object control matrix

DEVELOPING PROTOTYPE OBJECT DATA STRUCTURES

You can start by developing your object classes as data abstractions. Use the object-oriented information model to do this. What is your development environment? In C++, the definition for the ship object class would look like this:

```
class ship
{
    protected:
        int       number
        char*     name
        char*     owner
        int       ownerPhone
        char*     ownerAddress
}
virtual void ship :: assignShip ();
{ logic for assignShip service goes here }
```

In Smalltalk, the syntax would be:

```
class name            ship
superclass            Object
instance variables    number, name, owner, ownerPhone,
                      ownerAddress
class methods
assignShip
                      logic for assignShip service goes here
```

This is an appropriate time to stop and ask questions concerning tools. Do we really want to develop this prototype using an OOPL such as C++ or Smalltalk? The answer depends, in part, on whether or not there is access to a C++ or Smalltalk class library that contains a ship object class that could be extended to meet the requirements. Prototyping through reuse and extensions of existing object classes is, for the first time, a practical reality with modern object-oriented languages. By all means, take advantage of this capability whenever possible.

On the other hand, if the ship object class is being created for the first time, the rapidity of making modifications to the object during the many iterations of prototype refinement must be considered. In C++ or Smalltalk, how fast can the object data structures, controls, and services be created and modified? To illustrate the type of development environment that works better for the Harbor Information System example than C++ or Smalltalk, we will select one that has a short learning curve and with which we are familiar. We will not spend much time on syntax specific to that environment, and ask the reader to be indulgent and imaginative as to how the general principles apply to any similar tool that might be selected.

We are going to create the Harbor Information System prototype with HyperCard. The procedures described below would be almost identical using either Gain Momentum or MetaCard on a Unix workstation and would be similar using any of the higher rated tools referenced in Chapter 4. Figure 5.7 shows what the HyperCard environment would look like if it were used to create the Ship object class. Using visual programming, rather than compilable syntax, the attributes and the data entry screen for entering the information about new Ship object instances are being created at the same time.

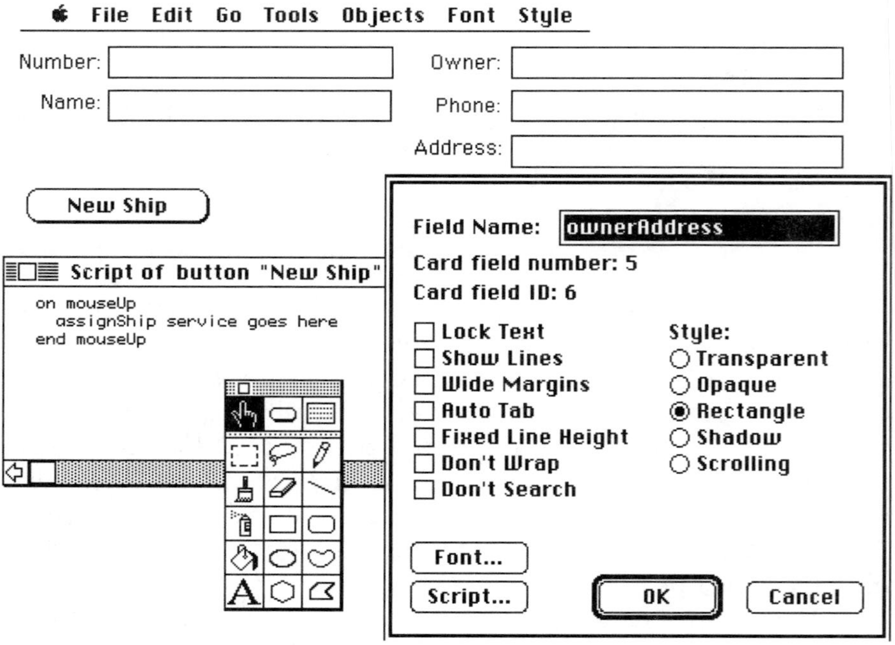

Figure 5.7: HyperCard environment

The first step would be to start up the HyperCard environment, create a new stack, name it "Ship" and then begin creating the ship attributes as background fields of the stack.

At the bottom left of the screen shown in Figure 5.7 is a floating tool palette with three icons at the top: a pointing finger, a rounded rectangle, and a rectangle with dots in it. The rectangle with dots represents a field, the rounded rectangle a button, and the pointing finger puts the screen you are creating into operational mode so that data can be entered into the fields you just created. When a new field (HyperCard's term for attribute) is created, a dialog box comes up with field design parameters as shown at the lower right of Figure 5.7. Filling it out as shown and clicking the OK button has two immediate results: the Ship object has a new attribute, ownerAddress, and a data entry box for this attribute appears on the Ship data entry screen.

Everything about the attributes created in a good rapid prototyping tool is totally flexible and as easy to modify as it was to create. In the case of HyperCard, selecting the field tool from the palette and double clicking on the data entry box for the attribute brings back the field design parameters dialog box, allowing changes to be made by selection. As can be seen, services (HyperCard scripts) can be encapsulated at the field level, perhaps made to execute when the cursor enters or leaves the field. Using the transparent field design choice, HyperCard drawing tools, and the Macintosh standard cut, copy, and paste commands, the data entry boxes can have any physical appearance desired.

To create the object classes for the Harbor Information System in HyperCard, we create a new stack for each object class shown on the object class model. Rather than create separate stacks for dinghy, sailboat, powerboat, and yacht, it might make sense to simply create these four derived subclasses as backgrounds within the Ship stack, since the extensions consist of only a single attribute.

Once a primitive data entry screen has been created for an object class, users can immediately begin to enter test data into persistent instances of that object. With HyperCard, the data entry screen is automatically created as part of the object class definition process. If files containing test data pertinent to the application exist, these files can and should be copied into the objects at this point. The users will have a much easier time evaluating the prototype if they can see object instances containing familiar application domain data on their screens. In HyperCard this could be accomplished by writing a HyperTalk script to read the external file and copy its records into instances of a prototype object. The main logic syntax of such a script would be something like: "put fileField n into stackField n" inside a double nested repeat loop where n varies from one to the number of fields. In all good rapid prototyping environments the syntax for such copy routines relies on specifying the target object, listing the attributes to be loaded in the sequence in which they appear on the external file, and specifying the directory path location of the source file.

For the Harbor Information System, an electronic version of the Candidate Profile list from the Acme Placement Agency can be obtained. This information can be copied into the Guard object class. The Harbor and Slip objects will have to be prepopulated, and users are usually willing to enter data about new ships as part of the initial prototype demonstration. Each object class should, however, have a service that will be used primarily by the developer, to copy its instances to an external file and/or copy an external file into instances of the object. This will allow the test data to be unloaded, object attributes to be modified, and the test data to be loaded back into the new object data structure quickly and easily during prototype iterations.

DEVELOPING PROTOTYPE SERVICES

After the attributes for all object classes have been implemented, they are half complete. They must all have services—at least minimum services for adding, modifying, and deleting object instances. Data entry screens must be created for the Harbor, Slip, Guard, and Ship objects. Using a HyperCard-type tool, this is already accomplished when the object attributes are defined.

The associative object classes, PatrolRound and RentalAgreement, need to provide services for linking the appropriate instances of their connected objects. The PatrolRound object class assigns Guards to Harbors, with timeIn and timeOut data for each instance, using the assignGuard service. This service is similar to a data entry screen and the basis for the service will again be automatically provided by HyperCard. More complex processing needs to be added, however, to query the PatrolRound object class as to the current assigned guard presence for particular shifts at particular harbors so that resource leveling can be accomplished by the harbor manager. The RentalAgreement object class makes similar links between its associated object instances, Slip and Ship, using the assignShip service which sends a message to the calcRent service to determine the monthly rent to be charged for a particular ship instance.

The above identified services provide the input side of the source/sink diagram requirements. In order to provide an interesting prototype for preliminary evaluation, the output side must be added: a payroll service (payGuards), a purchase order service (orderShoes), a billing service (billOwner), a productivity analysis service (rentPercent) and a security status monitoring service (monitorStatus).

Let's look at how just one of these services, billOwner, would be developed using a HyperCard-type tool. The developer would first double-click on the icon for the Ship object stack to make it active, then find a place to encapsulate the billOwner service. We recommend working at the stack level so that the service will be inherited by and available to all four derived classes of the ship base class: Sailboats, Powerboats, Yachts and Dinghies.

Note the selection, "Objects," on the menubar shown at the top of Figure 5.7. Select "Stack Info" from the objects menu. This presents a dialog box with a "Script" button. Clicking this button opens a window where the HyperTalk script can be entered for the billOwner service. This service will then be encapsulated in the Ship object. Begin the service with the message trap "on MonthEnd" as specified in the object control matrix. The last line of this service will be "end MonthEnd". Never mind for the moment how the MonthEnd message will be generated. We'll discuss prototype message control in the next session of this chapter.

The main logic of the billOwner HyperTalk script will be to access each instance of the Ship object, determine what slip and harbor the owner is renting by accessing the connected Slip and Harbor objects, determine the amount of rent currently payable, and produce a statement that includes the owner's name and billing address. This is done by creating temporary variables, local to the billOwner service, for the slip, harbor, and amount due information.

The service will look for instances of the RentalAgreement object that have a matching ship number, slip object instances with slip number matching those on the appropriate rental agreements, and harbor object instances with harbor number matching that of the appropriate slips. The HyperTalk syntax for such matching is to "put" the number of the current object into a temporary variable, "open" the target object, then "find" the temporary variable value in a specified attribute of the target object—three simple lines of high-level OOPL.

Once the service performs the required matching, amounts due can be obtained from the RentalAgreement object, slip attributes from the Slip object, and harbor attributes from the Harbor object. For each instance of the Ship object, this information will be "put" into associated temporary variables and used to print a bill to send the owner. The report formatting can be done using HyperCard's visually programmable (click-and-drag the attributes) report writer, or by writing an external report file with HyperTalk.

The above description of service development gives an idea of how quickly and easily prototype services can be created with an advanced, high-level, object-oriented development environment such as HyperCard. There are several environments for all kinds of workstations that provide similar capabilities to quickly create easy-to-modify services using visual programming tools and powerful yet simple object-oriented syntax. Since the type of workstations available to an organization are often established, a tool that runs in that development environment and provides these features should be chosen.

In addition to the billOwner service, this tool may be used to develop the following nontrivial services for the initial prototype: assignShip, calcRent, rentPercent, orderShoes, payGuards, assignGuard, and monitorStatus. They are each to be developed from within their respective objects, as shown on the object class model, so that they will be encapsulated there.

DEVELOPING PROTOTYPE OBJECT CONTROL MECHANISMS

With attributes and services in place, a working prototype is almost in existence. All that is lacking is a way for the user to operate the prototype in order to evaluate its features. The components of the prototype created so far represent system requirements—what the system must do in terms of capturing data, and producing information. The components that must be created in order to provide users with a working prototype will represent a system design—how the system will work in a specific technological setting.

Consider for a moment the differences that might exist between the prototyping environment and the operational environment. Will the user workstations have the same capabilities as the developer workstations? If so, then no worries. Often, however, economics dictate that the developers may have powerful intelligent workstations while users will get dumb terminals connected to a host computer. At other times developers have to use workstations less powerful than those the users will eventually get, because the acquisition for the components of the new distributed computing environment are not yet complete. Perhaps autonomous embedded software is under development, dictating almost no user interface in the final system. In these cases, the danger is that a user interface can be created during rapid prototyping that may not be easy to recreate in the operational environment. This is something to be aware of, but don't let it make or break the rapid prototyping approach.

Too often rapid prototyping is characterized as being primarily a user interface definition approach. The user interface is important, and working out its details is one of the possible benefits to be derived from rapid prototyping. But that should not overshadow the fact that rapid prototyping is a total requirements discovery technique. In a situation where it is not easy to rapidly prototype the operational user interface on the development workstation, concentration can be on data capture, data transformation, and information output functional requirements. Don't try too hard to please the user with the prototype interface. This will be a throwaway prototype, useful as a dynamic model of functional requirements, but not evolvable into operational software.

In any case, a user interface of some sort is needed in order to allow the user to experiment with and evaluate the prototype. So let's create a user interface for the HyperCard prototype of the Harbor Information System to see how this might be done in a high-level development environment. One way is to create a startup screen that would provide some system-level help for first-time users and choices of available services for all users. In HyperCard, a new stack called "MainMenu" with a "Help" button, a "Reports" button, a "New Things" button, and an "Operations" button could be created. Alternately, these could be choices on a "HIS" (Harbor Information System) menu item on the menu bar. Figure 5.8 shows what such a screen might look like.

Creating the MainMenu screen is trivial. What goes in the services encapsulated in this design object class is message generators to access other object classes and their services. Maybe other menu and system screen object classes should be created so that when the user clicks the "Operations" button, a screen appears offering the choices, "Assign Guards," "Assign Ships," "End Contract," and "Monitor Status." Clicking the "New" button would allow selection of data entry services for Guards, Ships, Slips, or Harbors. Clicking the "Reports" button would allow selection of "Payroll," "Shoe Order," "Monthly Bills," and "Profitability." The message generators in the HyperCard buttons on the main menu screen open the stacks created to display the help, reports menu, data entry menu, and op-

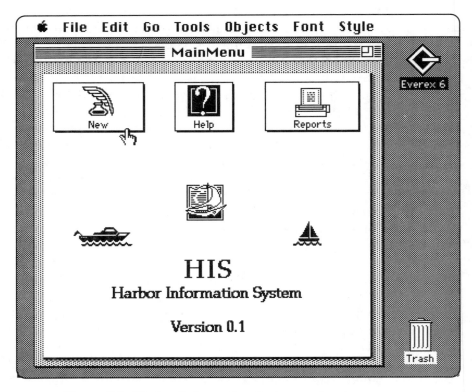

Figure 5.8: Harbor Information System main menu screen

erations menu screens. The syntax is simple. The "Reports" button on the main menu, for instance will contain the three line script:

```
on mouseUp,
     go stack "reportsMenu"
end mouseUp
```

The reports menu is another one-card stack (one instance object) displaying a screen with buttons to select desired reports. At this level, clicking on a choice will generate one of the messages on the object control matrix. Clicking the button labeled "Profitability," for instance, will invoke the script:

```
on mouseUp,
     go stack "Slip"
     monthEnd
end mouseUp
```

The Slip object class will then trap the monthEnd message. The Slip object class was made active by the above message generator. Slip contains the rentPercent service, which is a message handler that begins with the line "on monthEnd". In actual operation, the harbor manager wants the rentPercent service to run automatically each month. This is not difficult to do, simply encapsulate a service in the main menu that checks the date and has the necessary logic to access the Slip object class and generate the monthEnd message at the end of every month. The same main menu service can access the Guard object class and generate a payday message every Friday in order to activate the PayGuards service.

For the initial prototype, it might be best for buttons on a reports menu to generate the messages needed to run each report: The reports can be run easily on demand for evaluation. In fact, the prototype can demonstrate both, and if the user does not want the buttons in the final system, they may be simply deleted after the reports are working perfectly.

The menu objects created so far were not specified in the object class model described at the beginning of this chapter, because they can be created with a good prototyping tool faster than they can be specified. How they work is also self-documenting. If documentation is really needed for menus, the menu design documentation can be derived from the user-approved prototype when the prototype iteration phase is over.

The object control matrix is used to specify messages and how they are trapped by services in ways that are not always transparent when operating the prototype. It tells you, for instance, that when the monthEnd message is generated, the RentalAgreement object class must execute the calcRent service, the Ship object class must execute the billOwner service, and the Slip object class must execute the rentPercent service. This is easy to accomplish from a button on the reports menu. Simply modify the service above that generates the monthEnd message to read:

```
on mouseUp,
      go stack "RentalAgreement"
      monthEnd
      go stack "Ship"
      monthEnd
      go stack "Slip"
      monthEnd
end mouseUp
```

After message-generating services have been created and encapsulated in user-controllable object classes based on the object control matrix, the Harbor Information System prototype is complete and ready to demonstrate to the harbor manager. The project at this point should be about one week old.

6

Refinement

This chapter presents a description of how the Harbor Information System can be evolved into a user-approved, fully documented application. This can be accomplished by iterative refinement of both the object-oriented specifications and the executable prototype. All development activities (analysis, design, code, and test) are performed concurrently during requirements definition using prototype iteration. Analysis and design specifications are updated during each iteration. Test planning is performed prior to each prototype demonstration, and the demonstration itself is a test of a fully integrated prototype.

Differences between this approach and the incremental development model or the spiral lifecycle model proposed by Barry Boehm are centered around the type of development tools used. The tools must create software and specifications that are so easy to modify that dozens of iterations can take place between demonstration of the initial prototype and user approval of the final version. These iterations are all contained within the requirements definition phase of the project in order to ensure that the important requirements have been captured in the final version of the prototype.

PROTOTYPE ITERATION

An object-oriented prototype is iterated as many times as necessary until functionality of the services, information requirements represented by the data attributes, and control structures represented by message generators are sanctioned by the requirements commissioners to be correct and complete. The actual number of iterations is typically at least 12 and sometimes more than 50, depending on application complexity, user difficulty, and robustness of the prototyping tool in use. The Rumbaugh method suggests that six iterations are normally sufficient, but our experience is that this will not produce a prototype that will be completely satisfactory to requirements commissioners.[1] If the prototype represents all software requirements approved by the requirements commissioners, and the specifications have been evolved concurrently, then the final requirements document may be published at the conclusion of prototype iteration.

For each iteration, the prototype is demonstrated to users in order to discover additionally required services, data attributes, and control mechanisms. During the demo, existing services, data attributes, and control mechanisms are also evaluated for correctness, and the graphical user interface is assessed. Beginning with the second prototype demonstration, an attempt is always made to verify that the problems discovered during the previous demonstration have been corrected.

Users have responsibilities during prototype iterations to

- attend regular prototype demonstrations;
- study output to find errors;
- provide constructive criticism and suggestions;
- identify additional requirements; and
- cooperate to converge on a requirements solution within schedule and budget.

User commitment to this level of participation is crucial. Without it, rapid prototyping may not be advisable. An alternate, but much less satisfactory approach is to employ non-users attempting to take the user's point of view, but this will not be totally satisfactory. There is no substitute for real user involvement.

Development should not continue past prototype iteration until users have expressly approved prototype correctness, completeness, and exactness. Documentation should provide everything needed for software maintenance of the system components that exist at this point, as verified by maintenance personnel. Existing performance problems should be well documented and preliminary performance requirements specified so that solutions may be developed following completion of requirements definition.

Preparing for a Prototype Demonstration

The first step in prototype iteration is to prepare for a demonstration of the prototype to the user(s). A good technique is to create a script and rehearse it. A prototype demonstration script is very similar to and can be derived from Jacobson use cases;[2] it runs through one or more scenarios of how a user will actually use the software in his or her job. All new requirements, represented by the current version, should be demonstrated, as well as features that were corrected based on feedback from the previous demonstration.

The script should provide for a demo of one to two hours in length; the rehearsal should verify the timing. This way, the initial prototype may be evaluated: Was it too ambitious (overspecified); not ambitious enough (trivial); or just right (a one- to two-hour demo)? A one- to two-hour demo will usually provide just the right amount of feedback to give a two-person prototyping team a week's worth of work to do in refining the specifications and the prototype. A longer demo will cause users to lose interest during the demo, perhaps missing critical problems, and causing the project to lose momentum during long refinement periods.

A good demo script for an initial prototype might look something like the following:

- Show the start-up screen
- Invoke the application level help facility to explain the system overview
- Invoke the data entry screens for several object classes and allow the user to experiment with them
- If there are intermediate services (not data entry or output), invoke them and show the results to the user
- Show the outputs menu screen to user and invoke the output help facility
- Have the user actually invoke one or two reports and displays
- If there is a large hardcopy report, save it until the end, show how it is invoked, kill the print job and pass out copies that were printed prior to the demo

For the Harbor Information System (HIS) prototype created in the last chapter, the demo script could be the following:

- Ask the harbor manager to double-click on the HIS main menu stack, show her the Harbor Information System main menu screen.
- Have the harbor manager click the help button and look at the help screen while explaining the general workings of the prototype.
- Return to the main menu and click the Data Entry button. Have the user invoke each of the choices: Harbor, Patrol-Round, Guard, Slip, RentalAgreement, Ship, Sailboat, Powerboat, Yacht, and Dinghy. Encourage user to experiment with data entry into each object class.
- Have the user click the temporary Month End button to invoke the calcRent service. Retrieve the results from the appropriate RentalAgreement object instance.
- Invoke the Harbor Reports menu screen from the main menu and click on the report help button. Let the user read the help text.
- Have the user execute the payroll (payGuards service), billing (billOwner), and purchase order (orderShoes) outputs.
- Run the Profitability (rentPercent) report before the demo. Show the user how to invoke it from the reports menu and give her a copy of the report to study for errors.

Evaluating Prototype Object Attributes, Services, and Control Mechanisms

The prototype should be evaluated at each demonstration for completeness, correctness, and exactness. The evaluation should not be comprehensive, but simply an interchange to move development in a positive direction toward fulfillment of requirements. For completeness, ask the requirements commissioners to freely suggest desires for additional functionality, data management, and user interface controls and features (what else is needed?). For correctness, have them identify functions, information ouput, and controls that are not as desired (is there anything wrong?). For exactness, have them identify features that are not desired at all. Problems identified at the last demonstration must be corrected in the current version of the prototype (scrubbing unnecessary bells and whistles will excelerate development).

During the HIS demonstration, the harbor manager might have responded in this fashion:

- "Let the main menu stack be a customized icon (perhaps a picture of a harbor) residing on my main window, along with my word-processing icon and my spreadsheet icon."
- "I saw a program demonstrated the other day that had some of the menus appear as picture buttons on a toolbar across the top of the windows. As soon as I double-click the main executable icon, I would like to see a toolbar with pictures of menu items to choose from."
- "I like the Help shell, and maybe when I get used to the system, I may not need so much help, but for right now I would feel a lot more comfortable if every time I select something from the window (one click), I get some sort of explanation before I actually open it (two clicks)."
- "Just as with the main menu, I would prefer submenus (like the one for data entry) to be pictures that I can click rather than lists of words."
- "Somehow, it seems to me that Data Entry is a bit of a misnomer since that is the same place data is changed and deleted as well as entered."
- "It would make more sense to me if the Month End button were placed with other functions under some main function category."
- "I won't really be interested in PatrolRound unless I am thinking about guards. Could we lump them together?"
- "I view all reports as outputs, so would like to see the payroll, billing, and purchase order grouped together as information I get out of this system (as opposed to information I put into it)."
- "On the surface, the profitability report looks good and I see how to invoke it, but I will need to study it at my desk to be sure the figures are accurate."

- "Billing the ship owners is one of the most important aspects of my job. May I please witness some automatically generated bills at the next prototype demonstration?"

Prototype Refinement Based on User Feedback

Based on the harbor manager's feedback at the first prototype demonstration, the developer may realize the importance of the graphic user interface to this particular user. In response, the first task may be to worry a little less (for now) about the functionality and worry a little more about presentation style or *interface grammar*. The developer may want to begin by researching bit maps to use as icons. Clip art collections are available both as inexpensive commercial products and from the public domain. Graphic objects from these collections can easily be copied, pasted into the prototype screens, and customized to suit the application.

Create a picture, or some type of graphical representation for every object identified during the brief analysis phase—harbor, guard, ship (sailboat, powerboat, yacht, dinghy), slip, patrolRound, rental agreement, and so forth. In addition, menu icons for help, data manipulation, reports, and functions need to be explored, both for appropriate pictures and meaningful names for these categories that will label the message generators used to invoke the services provided by system objects.

Figure 6.1 describes the control hierarchy as the user will see it.

- An application system executable icon will exist on the user's desktop. When double-clicked, the icon will open to a main window where symbols at the top of the screen make up menu items in a toolbar.
- The icon for the help facility may be a large question mark— when double-clicked, the help dialog begins.
- An icon representing data (a grid-like spreadsheet perhaps?) is also on the toolbar—when double-clicked, another window with another toolbar menu appears.
- One of the selections on the data toolbar is the picture of a ship—when double-clicked, radio buttons for sailboat, powerboat, yacht, and dinghy appear.
- When a type of ship (an object) is selected, a screen of data appears (instances of the set of attributes for an object)—the user

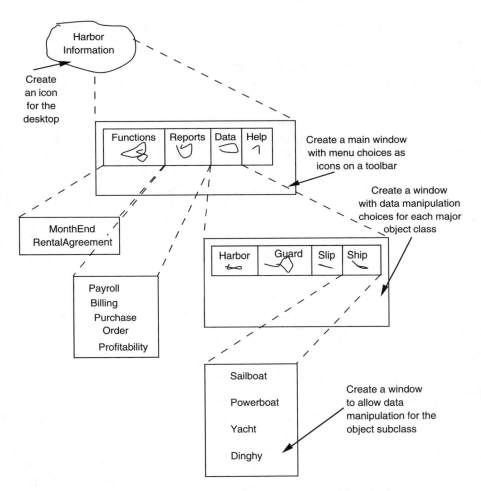

Figure 6.1: User view of application control hierarchy

may then insert instances (rows), delete instances (rows), or modify whole instances or individual attributes of instances (rows/columns).

- Because the harbor manager asked for context-sensitive help, a single click (selection) on any icon should result in a brief description somewhere on the screen, usually at the bottom.

In addressing the user interface issues, developers may take advantage of thousands of hours and millions of dollars spent in research on the psychological considerations of graphical user interfaces. Here are a few basics to keep in mind.

- Color is an important factor, but should be used sparingly. Hot dog stand colors become tiresome after the first few executions.

- Placement of controls is of vital importance, as is the consistency of the placement as the user moves between and among windows. EXIT buttons normally appear at the bottom of a screen, for example. For a given application, it may not matter so much where a particular control appears as that it appears in exactly the same place on every screen. Application-building tools make powerful use of inheritance in enforcing such consistency.

- Checkboxes and radio buttons are best used for the purpose they were intended. Checkboxes typically allow multiple choices where radio buttons are meant to indicate one choice among a group (e.g., male or female). To confuse the usage is to confuse and frustrate the user.

- Typically, command buttons and list boxes are used to initiate an action; checkboxes, radio buttons and list boxes are used to specify an option or value.

- There are some excellent publications for becoming acquainted with "windows grammar" and on-line "data choreography"[3,4]

There are other changes to be made to accommodate the harbor manager's response to the first prototype. Some functions simply need to be moved to appear on a more desirable access path. The only major change, in addition to the user interface, is to add functionality for automatic invoice creation. A second prototype demonstration should be ready in a couple of days, if the developer works on the project full-time.

Approval of Prototype-Demonstrated Requirements

The above loop—demonstration followed by feedback and refinement—will be repeated many times, until user confidence in the completeness, correctness, and exactness of the application is high and the remaining budget for requirements definition is low. It will then be time to publish the final requirements document and move on to the tuning, testing, and detailed design documentation that will be necessary in order to deliver the final product.

The tasks required to evolve a fully refined prototype into a deliverable application are covered in the next chapter. But first, how does one go about getting the requirements commissioners to approve an extensively refined version of the prototype? As Figure 6.2 shows, they will always want more. In fact, the routine of one-hour demos followed by one-week refinements tends always to create about one week's more work. This can continue indefinitely, and if the prototype is evolved into production software as described in the next chapter, quick easy refinements to the system can be made forever.

It is important, however, to get on with putting the system into production so that it can be used to do real work as opposed to mere experimentation. A deadline should have been set for this transition—a marketing window of opportunity or a critical organizational need. Rapid prototyping provides an easy way to meet such deadlines, because with a prototype, there is always a working system, the system is always incomplete to some extent, and that is always understood to be acceptable. Upon completion, the system may be said to be correct although possibly still incomplete.

One of the interesting phenomena of rapid prototyping is that,

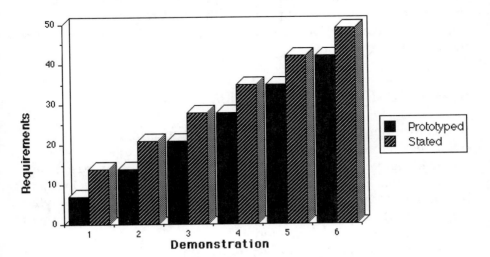

Figure 6.2: The more they get, the more they want

as prototype iterations proceed, the gap between stated requirements and demonstrated requirements narrows dramatically. Figure 6.2 shows that at the first iteration the demonstrated requirements will be about 50 percent of what the users say they want. At the sixth iteration about 90 percent of stated requirements will be met. On one two-year build, one of the authors did 53 prototype iterations in six months of requirements definition. At the end of this time, the gap between demonstrated requirements and stated requirements was less than 0.1 percent. At this point, requirements commissioners will actually become impatient with prototype iteration and demand that the system be put into production. Further enhancements can come later.

The secret to obtaining user approval of the final version of the requirements prototype is to put a deadline for obtaining this approval in the project plan. Make it clear in the plan that getting to the point where it is reasonable to approve the prototype is the responsibility of the entire team, both developers and requirements commissioners. Each iteration will bring the prototype closer to what the requirements commissioners want. A week or two before the deadline, hold a last chance demonstration. Make it clear at this event that this is the last opportunity the requirements commissioners will have, until after the system is put into production, to request refinements. The requirements definition is then understood to be complete if the prototype incorporates these last requests at the final demo. Using this approach, the worst slippage of the final requirements review will be maybe a week or two—just until the user's final wish list is incorporated.

OBJECT-ORIENTED DESIGN EVOLUTION

In a conventional approach to software engineering, there comes a point, just before writing the actual code, that the "code-to" design is finalized and approved. In formal, methododology-based approaches, this point occurs after about half of total development budget has been spent. Managers keep their fingers crossed, praying that the design will be easily implementable and that the users will be pleased with the implementation.

With incremental, iterative, rapid prototyping, as presented here, a working, user-approved system and a set of associated design specifications exist at this same point—halfway through the project. The difference is that, in the prototyping approach, there still has been no conventional procedural code written. In fact, it has been carefully avoided in order to keep the prototype easy to modify during the many iterations from initial demonstration to approval of the final version. As with all conceptual statements, there are times when some manifestations of reality vary from the theory, and some tools may require a small amount of programming in order to support the prototype. For instance, the object-oriented rapid prototyping tool XVT will probably require some procedural code in order to open and close windows and provide functionality such as data manipulation (add, change, delete). Yet, as a rule, procedural code proliferation in the prototype stage will be kept to a minimum.

When the requirements commissioners have approved all features and functions of the prototype, policies about developing software in procedural languages can be relaxed. A low-level procedural language might be needed in order to get the required performance from some of the more computationally intensive or data-laden user-approved functions. In these cases, it will be advisable to have the same quantity and quality detailed design documentation as for a conventional development project. In other words, now a conventional code-to design document is needed. Fortunately, such a document almost exists, in the prototype specification, assuming that the spec has been kept up to date with each prototype iteration. The following steps describe what remains to be done to complete an adequate code-to detailed design.

The first step is to review compiled notes on performance phenomenon observed during prototype demonstrations and experimentation. The users will have provided plenty of feedback about performance and it should have been recorded. Studying these notes will distinguish which object class services are most likely to need performance tuning. These then are the object classes to which the most detailed design attention should be directed.

Here is a list of the detailed design documentation that should exist for an adequate code-to design of an object class:

- Graphics that model interaction of complex services, where those services are represented at the atomic program unit level
- Service specifications to the pseudo-code or PDL level

- Physical data dictionary definitions of class attributes
- Allocation of object classes to hardware architecture
- Performance thread analysis

Program unit graphics could consist of various kinds of graphic models of the interaction of complex services in a usage scenario. Different methodologies have different recommendations about how to represent such a design component graphic. In structured methods, this was typically the structure chart that described the module hierarchy and coupling. Since the choice of such a representation will have no effect on how rapid prototyping is done, we have no preference and encourage the use of whatever approach is recommended by the methodology in play (a partial list was presented in Chapter 3.[1,5,6] Specifications for complex services, where conventional programs are anticipated, should also include pseudo code or program description language. If, however, a declarative OO 4GL, such as HyperTalk, has been used to script prototype services, the scripts themselves are sufficient service specifications.

Physical data definitions include whatever information is required, including data type and format, to implement persistent objects as file or database table structures. In highly distributed applications, the object classes may be spread among multiple computers, often in peer-to-peer relationships. During the early stages of prototyping, it isn't necessary to even know what these computers are. But, as one moves toward final implementation and works toward understanding and meeting all performance requirements, a software/hardware architecture diagram that shows what goes where should emerge. Object classes should be shown on this diagram, attached to their respective computers.

Finally, each service should be examined to determine which services, if any, must execute before this one can provide its intended function and which services, if any, will normally execute upon its termination. This type of analysis produces performance threads. Determine what the requirements commissioners' budget is for time allowed to complete each thread, and document these budgets as the performance requirements of the system. Note that this effort cannot be completed until it is known, from discovery through prototyping, what all the services are and what they must do. Simply saying that all services must have subsecond execution time and all performance threads must complete within 200 milliseconds (we have seen this kind of specification many times), is overly simplistic, may not be achievable, and is unnecessary in many cases. Specifying performance requirements before functional requirements have been defined will, at best, unnecessarily drive up development costs. It is this sort of understanding, grown from experience, that makes rapid prototyping a valid approach, even though performance-inefficient advanced development environments (perhaps utilizing interpreted OO 4GLs) are employed.

All of the documentation that will be needed for conventional software maintenance is now in place. Software maintenance (as opposed to rapid prototyping) can be defined as making changes to a finished system. That is exactly what will be undertaken during final testing and performance tuning. It would be advisable to conduct structured walkthroughs of this documentation at this point and to have the walkthrough teams staffed by maintenance professionals—the people who are likely to be saddled with the responsibility of maintaining the application after it is delivered and put to use.

ENDNOTES

1. Rumbaugh, J., Blaha, M., Premerlni, W., Eddy, F., and Lorensen, W., *Object-Oriented Modeling and Design*, Englewood Cliffs, NJ: Prentice-Hall, 1991.

2. Jacobson, I., Christerson, Jonsson, and Overgaard, *Object-Oriented Software Engineering: A Use Case Driven Approach*, Addison-Wesley, Wokingham, England, 1992.

3. *The Windows Interface Guide*, Redmond, WA: Microsoft Press, 1992.

4. Sarna, D., and Febish, G., *Windows Rapid Application Development*, Emeryville, CA: Ziff-Davis Press, 1993.

5. Graham, I., *Object-Oriented Methods*, Wokingham, England, Addison-Wesley, 1994.

6. Booch, G., *Object-Oriented Analysis and Design with Applications*, Redwood City, CA: Benjamin Cummings, 1993.

7

Evolution

TO EVOLVE OR NOT TO EVOLVE?

A prototype may serve strictly as a dynamic requirements model and never evolve into a production-quality system. It may make sense to prototype with a tool like HyperCard, refine the prototype based on user feedback, and then entirely rewrite the application in C++. This would be a good approach if, for instance, the application is being developed for a computer for which there are no good prototype development tools but there is a good C++ compiler. Unfortunately, the effort involved in prototype development and refinement may appear to requirements commissioners to be in addition to total development costs. In actuality, those *extra* costs represent improved specifications, an investment that will have a substantial payoff in terms of user satisfaction and reduced rework after delivery of the final application.

In order to evolve into a production system *without* reprogramming, a prototype must be developed using advanced tools that will be available in the target as well as in the development hardware environment. A good prototype does not necessarily make a good production application. Many times, the prototype, if not completely rewritten after the requirements gathering process, must at least undergo some evolutionary tuning.

STRESS-TESTING APPROVED PROTOTYPE OBJECTS

From the perspective of persistent data storage, the attributes of object classes are similar to small flat file database management systems. This is so because the services of an object are frequently used to store persistent instances of an object, each with its own unique attribute values. At other times, a service is used to retrieve sets of object instances, based on some criteria, another database type of function. Perhaps multiple users will want to concurrently add, retrieve, and modify object instances—usage typical of database systems. Even in cases where object instances do not get stored and no user access occurs, there may be a data management performance problem resulting from a requirement to process large volumes of incoming object instances received from some external device or system.

Two classical data management problems are large numbers of concurrent user accesses and large volumes of data to be processed. During prototype iteration the maximum possible number of users are not typically involved, nor is the maximum volume of production application data readily available. Developers usually work with only one or two requirements commissioners who are testing user access. Developers typically test with only a representative sample of application data. It makes perfect sense to delay performance issues until the prototype is approved. Until such time, performance concerns are premature since the functionality is still emerging. However, once the functionality is approved, it's time to worry about performance issues.

To determine whether there are or will be performance problems, it is necessary to stress-test all parts of the application. Fortunately, due to encapsulation, object classes are easier to stress-test than structured application modules. Simply take each object class that will store persistent data and load it with increasing amounts of data (by creating persistent instances with copy scripts) until performance of its services becomes unacceptable to the users. Take each object class that will experience multi-user access and have increasing numbers of users execute concurrent trial retrieval services until performance becomes unacceptable. Take each object class that must process data coming in from an external device and test it with the real device in conditions that maximize the incoming data volume. Requirements commissioners will know which object classes do not meet performance requirements. These are the object classes that exhibit unacceptable performance before maximum expected data and usage volumes are reached. These object classes may be considered *broken* and must be fixed before the application is of production quality.

Note that the performance of object services is largely a function of two factors outside of the developer's control: the number of

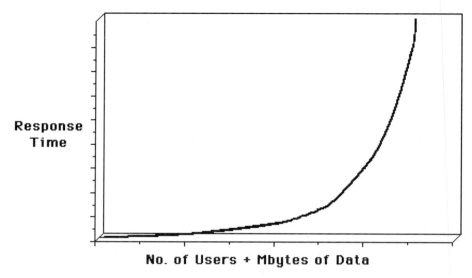

Figure 7.1: Execution time as a function of users and data

object instances and the number of users concurrently accessing an object class. As Figure 7.1 shows, these two factors combine to increase service execution time. This provides two clues as to how to accomplish effective stress-testing.

First, performance will be fairly steady, as users and data increase, up to the breaking point, where suddenly execution time will start to increase dramatically. Second, after determining the breaking point caused by too much data, and, separately, the breaking point caused by too many users, tests should be conducted to increase users and data concurrently, according to some realistic ratio. Fortunately, it is not necessary to determine the precise level of users or data that the object classes will support. The results of a stress test will produce data from which the developer may make an informed judgment about tolerance ranges, and determine a threshold below which the object services will be considered unacceptable.

PERFORMANCE TUNING OBJECTS

After stress-testing, you will have a list of broken object services that are unacceptable because they exhibit poor performance. This situation dictates that object services get fixed so that required execution time is met. Numerous techniques may be used to meet the performance goals. If parts of the prototype were developed using high-level, interpreted, scripting languages, these are often the broken parts. There will then be an obvious temptation to rewrite all these parts in a lower-level, compilable programming language, so that the resulting executable object code will be much faster than the original interpreted script. Resist this temptation! Pursue all avenues for obtaining acceptable performance while retaining the easy modifiability of the high-level scripting language in order to reduce future maintenance costs.

A worthy goal during prototype evolution is to keep the production system just as easy to modify as the prototype, without sacrificing users' performance requirements. These five strategies for performance tuning are presented and discussed:

- Object class data structure optimization
- Hardware configuration modifications
- Distributing object classes across a network architecture
- Minimizing database overhead
- Lower-level language programming

These strategies are listed in order of easiest and most desirable first and least desirable last. Reprogramming in a lower-level language should always be the last resort, to be used when there is no other way to get the desired performance. Even then, only the services that are broken need be rewritten; everything else may be left alone. Just because reprogramming will make an application run faster doesn't mean speed is always a good trade-off for easy modifiability. Remember that maintenance is more than half of the software dollar and that users are often satisfied with greater than subsecond response when their interface and functionality are excellent.

Object Class Data Structure Optimization

Using the object class model, look at the area of the application that surrounds a broken object class. Is the broken object class in a deep inheritance hierarchy? Is the broken service trying to retrieve datasets that are combinations of data from several object classes? Are queries run on attributes that are always unique, but are not indexed or key fields? A yes answer to any of these questions identifies an opportunity for making simple changes that will improve performance.

In most object-oriented environments, inheritance has an associated performance overhead. Derived object classes take time and memory to acquire the inherited attributes and services of their ancestor before making use of them. The benefits of inheritance are often touted, but performance degradation is the down side. A performance-improving technique during prototype evolution is to examine the number of attributes and services added to the inherited object by the derived class containing the poorly performing service. If it's only one or two attributes or a very small service, consider combining those attributes and services back into the base class and eliminating the derived class. In other words, flatten the hierarchy of the inheritance structure, or *promote* a descendant. Inheritance is desirable only within the limits dictated by performance constraints.

If a service always requires data from several object classes in order to provide its required output, the design is probably too tightly coupled in this area. Try moving some attributes from one object class to another, or combining two or more small object classes into one larger object class. The fastest data retrieval will always occur when an object's service needs data only from its own instances. When data from another object must be combined, the matching process slows down performance. If several objects must match multiple instances in a single output record, the result can be extremely slow execution time. This in an area where the conventional wisdom of information engineering is legitimately compromised. Well-encapsulated, loosely coupled object classes do not always adhere to the third normal form model of information engineering. If you learn to design with more encapsulation and looser coupling during prototype development, you will end up with less tuning to do after user approval of the prototype.

Finally, examine the logic in the poorly performing services. If string pattern matching, such as: attributeName = "String," is being used to select object instances in where clauses or conditional statements, and the values of attributeName are usually unique for each object instance, performance could be improved by building an index for this attribute into the object class definition.

Hardware Configuration Modifications

Sometimes, because of the high cost of software engineering labor, the cheapest and fastest way to improve the performance of applications is to upgrade the power of the machine being used to host the application. This may not apply as easily to decentralized, distributed, client/server environments. It is also a sad truth that hardware procurements in many organizations are hampered by bureaucratic red tape and politics—filling out forms, writing and rewriting justifications, performing cost/benefit studies, and making presentations to committees. Programmers, analysts, and designers cost the same amount of money whether they are developing programs or writing procurement justifications. Sometimes it is more cost effective to try to get along with whatever hardware configuration currently exists.

In other cases, it makes sense to try for the hardware upgrade. Most of the other tuning strategies involve sacrificing something good about the system, such as easy modifiability. If only the actual hardware cost is considered, and not the labor hours involved in the procurement effort (which can vary widely), upgrading may be cheaper than paying for programmer labor to get equivalent performance improvement. Upgrading hardware during final prototype tuning, just before putting new software into production, is the exact time upgrading makes most sense.

Get disks with faster access time. Get a CPU with faster clock speed. Get more CPU memory to cut down on the amount of swapping going on. Get faster memory. Get a RISC-based machine or a parallel processor. If users are accessing the application or pulling data across a local area network, see if their connection can be upgraded, for example, from simple, low-cost, personal computer LAN to ethernet, or from ethernet to fiber optic. Don't design the system to the lowest common denominator.

Distributing Object Classes across a Network Architecture

Distributed architectures are tricky, but not as tricky using object-oriented technology as they are for distributed relational databases. Databases like to be centralized, and when distributed, data integrity problems are created. Objects are, by nature, independent and don't mind where on a network of distributed processors they live relative to the objects with which they will collaborate. Messages can be sent to objects on other computers using remote procedure calls. Message parameters can be used to send and fetch data to and from the remote objects. If an object can be hosted on a decentralized workstation, as opposed to executing on a centralized server or mainframe, performance of the entire system may improve. Some prototyping tools, like PowerBuilder, assist by allowing for flexible creation of executable and dynamic libraries.

There are different strategies for object distribution. A common approach is to host graphic user interface (GUI) objects on the user workstations and put objects with computationally intensive services on a more powerful centralized server or mainframe. Another common practice is to distribute copies of all objects (the entire application) to each workstation as well as the server, then have periodic data collection services store accumulated new or modified data on the server.

Some tools allow for freedom of object distribution and a library search path to accommodate searching for more frequently used objects. A more complex strategy might involve distributing a large number of objects over a large number of workstations so that the application would execute in a peer-to-peer architecture. Which architecture will yield the required performance level with the least cost and effort will depend very much on the nature of the application, the software tools in play and the type of hardware being used. The simplest of these approaches, in terms of design complexity, is usually to put the GUI only on the client workstations, and the rest of the application on a centralized server. Using the simplest approach is perfectly acceptable, if it will meet the user's performance requirements.

Minimizing Database Overhead

Databases can be slow in comparison to the other pieces of the object-oriented computing picture. Queries are processed while you wait (and wait, and wait). When relational databases first became popular, they immediately acquired a reputation for sluggish performance—a reputation they have never entirely lived down, despite vendor efforts at improvement. Object-oriented databases appear to be much faster than relational systems. They often prove to have adequate performance for even many CAD (computer-aided design) and real-time applications. This is at least in part because object classes are not necessarily fully normalized and therefore performance degrading joins are not as common in an object-oriented application. When object-oriented database management systems are used as part of rapid prototyping environments, less performance tuning is necessary. This is particularly true when good (loosely coupled, well-encapsulated) object classes have been designed. There is a distinct similarity to building prototypes on top of a relational database designed according to conventional information engineering principles.

Even object-oriented databases will have some overhead associated with them. It will probably take just slightly longer to retrieve a selection of object instances from a single class in an object-oriented database than it will to retrieve the same set from an indexed file. Normally, the advantages of using a good data management system outweigh the disadvantage of paying a small performance price. If, however, the price is high (there is a big difference in retrieval time between the database object class and a file), move the data out to a file and revise the object services to add, modify, and delete persistent object instances to and from the file. Do this only for object classes that have broken services. Don't fix object classes that aren't broken.

Lower-Level Language Programming

When the tuning strategies listed above have been tried, yet some services still don't execute fast enough to meet user requirements, there is still *the last resort*—rewrite the service (not necessarily the entire class) in a lower-level language. If the service is in an interpreted fourth-generation OO language such as Gain Momentum's GEL, try replacing it with a compiled executable written in an object-oriented language such as C++. If you're already in C++, and it's too slow, try making a call to a compiled function written in C or even assembler. This technique of dropping down to lower-level languages only where nothing else will produce the required performance will not give you the fastest application around, but it will give you a fast enough application that also retains maximum ease of modification. If everything has been tried, including dropping down to assembler, and a service still won't run fast enough, the only thing left to adjust is the user's expectations. It is not always possible to get subsecond response time with very large numbers of users accessing very large amounts of data.

Tuning Techniques for a Specific Environment

PowerBuilder, used in a client/server Microsoft Windows environment, is an excellent rapid prototyping tool. It interfaces with several database management systems, including, ALLBASE/SQL™, DB2™, INFORMIX™, ORACLE™, SQLBase™, SQL Server™, and

XDB™. It will support Microsoft's Open DataBase Concept (ODBC™), which will enable PowerBuilder applications to access a variety of other databases including Rdb™, Ingres™, and SQL/400™. New database interfaces will probably be added on a regular basis. The following is a list of techniques to consider when tuning an evolved prototype built using PowerBuilder. At this writing, WATCOM™ may be purchased bundled with the PowerBuilder product. All products undergo continual change. This list is a snapshot in time of currently recommended tuning strategies for PowerBuilder, a tool which will grow more robust with future releases.

- Because PowerBuilder is so tightly coupled to a database, optimization of the object-oriented information model is crucial, performing the same role the Entity-Relationship Diagram (ERD) has played in conventional database design.
- Denormalization from third normal form back to second or even first normal form may be necessary to meet production performance needs.
- For any object instance, PowerBuilder maintains, in memory, one object class definition for the ancestor chain. It is recommended that no more than three to four levels of inheritance be used.
- Maximize use of instantiation. Once the inheritance chain is invoked and consuming resources, use those definitions as many times as possible.
- Minimize network traffic. Aggregate data at the database server whenever possible.
- Limit the number of connect occasions from the client to the database. They increase network traffic, are slow and resource-consuming. In addition to performance issues, there are associated user satisfaction issues. A user will wait patiently for a connect at application start-up and will express dissatisfaction at the prospect of a delay during application use.
- Perform frequent updates. New and modified data may be shipped from the client to the database server over the network in small bursts. This approach is preferable to tying the network up for long periods of time, running the risk of contention, and running the risk of more work when rollbacks are required.

- Perform as much data validation at the client as possible to unburden the server of processing cycles and ultimately reduce network traffic.
- Use the database optimizer.
- Control scoping of variables. Resist the temptation to use global variables. They are convenient in that they are available to all scripts in an application, but they are not object-oriented (they violate encapsulation) and they degrade performance.
- Use data windows whenever possible. They make better use of Windows resources than do controls.
- Minimize the use of redraw.
- Limit libraries to about 800K.
- Structure library search paths such that reusable objects, which should be in use most often, are earliest in the search path.
- Consider the proper mix of executables versus dynamic libraries. Performance may be enhanced by placing more frequently used object libraries into executables and less frequently used objects into dynamic libraries.

IS IT READY FOR SHRINK-WRAP?

After tuning, application software will exist that the requirements commissioners like that meets performance requirements. It is the time when commercial software vendors might copy the application disks and put them in shrink-wrap plastic for sale. If it is custom software developed for in-house use, it might be time to put the application on users' workstations or in the production account of the mainframe and tell users it's ready for use. The following is a short checklist to see if this is really a production-quality system, or just a prototype.

✓Did the requirements commissioners formally give written approval of the latest version of the prototype as an acceptable model of requirements?

This is always the primary goal of a prototyping project—make the customer happy! Avoid becoming disillusioned with object-oriented rapid prototyping just because the requirements commissioners cannot accept one of the prototype versions. Such unhappiness could be caused by many factors, such as bad estimates, requirements changes, environment changes, organization structure changes, and organizational politics. Chapter 10 provides object-oriented metrics for sizing and estimating object-oriented rapid prototyping projects. These metrics can be applied to setting a realistic date for the end of prototype iteration.

✓Has the user formally approved the performance of the final application at maximum probable stress levels?

Because stress-testing and performance tuning take place after the requirements commissioners have approved the prototype for functionality, for data management, and for control requirements, it is often easy to overlook formal approval of the performance of all services from the requirements commissioners. Get them to assume the risk of any future performance problems, or continue tuning. It is also necessary to assure that any services rewritten in lower-level languages still meet the commissioners' functional requirements.

✓Is the application adequately documented?

Will maintenance programmers have what they need to understand the application well enough to make efficient modifications when necessary? Will new users have the help they need to understand the workings of the system? Peer reviews can determine the answers to these questions conclusively. The project plan should have specified every piece of documentation to be produced. The project plan should have been certified by a peer review team for completeness and reasonableness. Each piece of documentation should then have been subjected to peer review at completion.

It is a good idea to have maintenance staff on the peer review team. This way they get a preview of the evolving new product and can address maintainability issues. Also, they can make sure that the documents being produced will be what is needed to understand and modify the delivered software. It will also be an indicator of whether or not the maintenance staff has adequate skills and training to work with software that may have been developed using new technology.

There are those who believe that a new set of team roles is necessary when developing and maintaining object-oriented systems using rapid prototyping in a modern environment. These roles, in addition to the requirements commissioners, include project leader, network architect, database administrator, prototyping tool expert, and object class library manager. In an application where the end user controls processing sequence, the software essentially loses control and becomes a collection of appropriate responses to user stimulus. Documentation can become a nightmare without the object class manager. He or she must ensure that the object class model, the object control matrix, and the service specifications remain in sync with the way the system works. Without the serial control of procedural systems and without the proper documentation, the maintainer may have difficulty determining the details of what happens when various messages are issued or where to look when problems occur.

MAINTAINING OBJECT-ORIENTED PROTOTYPE-DEVELOPED SOFTWARE

When the new software requires a maintenance fix or enhancement, the modification can be treated as if it were simply another prototype iteration. Do version control at the object class level. Check out an object class for modification. Check out the effected subject area portion of the object class model. Make any needed changes, for example, a new service is required, to the model. Then prototype the change. Use prototyping tools to make the change. Demonstrate the change to the requirements commissioners. Perhaps a few iterations and a new stress test will be necessary for complex modifications. When the modified class meets all requirements, increment the version number and check it back into the baseline. Keep a separate version number for the entire application and increment it every time any object class gets modified.

To the extent that the application stays easy to modify during the tuning phase of development, maintenance modifications will be just as easy and just as fast as prototype iterations were. Good rapid prototyping means rapid prototyping forever—iteration and refinement are never done.

8

Lifecycles

MODIFYING SEQUENTIAL LIFECYCLES

This chapter discusses how the activities undertaken and products produced in an object-oriented rapid prototyping project are different from those produced in a conventional sequential lifecycle approach. It is important to know what activities and deliverables are critical, and it is also good to know how to tailor existing lifecycle standards to allow object-oriented approaches to work better.

For the purpose of discussion, we will use the sequence of activities shown in Figure 8.1 to represent a typical conventional sequential lifecycle. The white dot represents the start of an activity or lifecycle phase; the black dot indicates completion. The forward arrow indicates that information produced in one phase is fed forward and used as the basis for work in the following phase. The backward arrow indicates that discoveries made during later phases can sometimes require changes to work previously completed. Unfortunately, some organizations continue to follow this model. The tragic flaw, of course, is that discoveries made during the final hours of testing (user acceptance testing) often require that the majority of work done during all the previous phases be extensively revised. When this happens, which is most of the time using this approach, all the work up to this point amounts to nothing more than one very expensive prototype iteration.

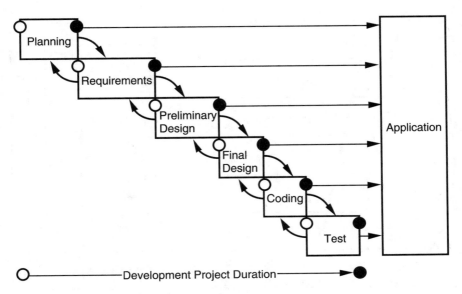

Figure 8.1: The bad old sequential lifecycle

A LIFECYCLE COMPATIBLE WITH OORP

Most modern software engineering methodologies recognize that a more feasible, successfully repeatable, lifecycle process is incremental, concurrent, and iterative. Figure 8.2 illustrates such a lifecycle. Each new phase is allowed to begin very shortly after the previous phase has begun. Requirements analysis begins, based on a tiny bit of preliminary planning. A tiny set of requirements and design models are sufficient to begin development of prototype code. If developers are asked what they are doing at any point during such a project, they will probably say that they are doing a little bit of everything: concurrent analysis, design, prototype development, and testing. If they are asked when a particular activity, such as requirements analysis will be complete, the same answer is given for any activity—at the end of the project.

As previous material has explained and experience has shown, the lack of sequentialism is a cause for celebration, not concern, in an object-oriented rapid prototyping approach. Just because we do everything concurrently, there is no reason why we can't use a formalized approach with appropriate configuration management, planning, and progress measurement. Chapter 10 explains how the total number of object classes can be estimated, based on very rapid

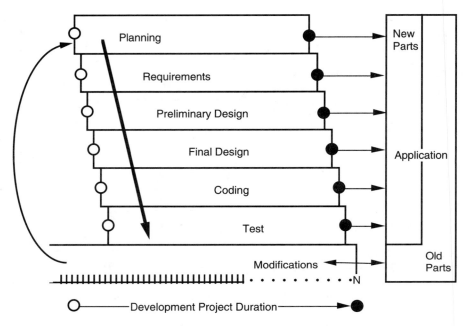

Figure 8.2: The new object-oriented Lifecycle

analysis during preliminary planning, and then how the effort required to model, develop, and test those objects can be derived. Then, if there is an estimate of 378 object classes for the final product, and there are 201 finished object classes in the current version of the prototype, we are probably more than 50 percent complete.

There is a line of N modifications running along the lifecycle timeline in Figure 8.2. This indicates that there will be many increments of additional requirements, additional design specification, additional development, and additional testing of new increments as new requirements are discovered, added, and tested as a result of prototype iterations. At some point, the last prototype iteration will occur and the requirements will be complete. Shortly afterwards, the detailed design specifications will be complete. When the last performance-tuned object class has been thoroughly tested, the application is ready for production use.

This new lifecycle concept is presented this way, because it becomes obvious that the activities and milestones for a rapid prototyping project are exactly the same as the activities and milestones of a project without rapid prototyping. There does not need to be a special lifecycle for rapid prototyping. The differences for rapid proto-typing will be the greater number of iterations that may be per-formed in a given amount of time using better prototyping tools, and the amount of user involvement in requirements and design def-inition. Using object-oriented development languages and good object-oriented design, you can iterate considerably because of the change-resilient nature of object-oriented software. With advanced object-oriented prototyping tools, as discussed in Chapter 4, dozens of incremental prototype versions may be prepared for demonstra-tions during requirements definition, as shown in Figure 8.2.

There is one other distinction that should be made regarding the new versus the old lifecycle. Figure 8.1 illustrates the assumption implied by all sequential software engineering processes—that everything about a development project is new. This has not been true for some time. Almost all modern applications are built on a foundation of existing software. As object class repositories grow, this trend may be expected to strengthen. Therefore, Figure 8.2 shows the new application consisting of old and new parts, with the majority being old and modifications being made to both over many iterations.

PRODUCTS OF THE OORP LIFECYCLE

In educating managers, customers, and developers about the impor-tance of getting the requirements right in order to make sure an ele-gant, well-designed, solution to the wrong problem would not be de-veloped, methodologists used to stress the difference between requirements analysis and design. Analysis provides a description of what the system does, and design describes how the system meets its requirements. Concurrent engineering, object-oriented methods, and rapid prototyping all conspire to blur the distinction between re-quirements specification and design specification to the point of meaninglessness. Modern specifications are leaning toward a single document approach—a product specification.

A product specification may have a requirements section and a design section, but for an object-oriented product, the contents of both sections will look very similar. Object-oriented models will be the primary content of the requirements section. The models will specify the problem domain objects. There will also be a strong hint of how the requirements will be accomplished as message passing is also modeled, and the model of each object class can be directly translated into software with an object-oriented development tool or language. The design section will simply contain more of the same kinds of objects, providing whatever is necessary to make the application work with a specific technology. When prototyping, it is obvious that the design models must be developed concurrently, that it will often be difficult to decide whether an object class belongs in the requirements or the design section of the specification. The distinction is becoming so artificial that it scarcely makes any difference.

Figure 8.3 shows how specific products are the result of specific lifecycle activities. Even though all activities are perfectly concurrent, they are still performed individually. We still do requirements analysis, and the result is a set of OOA models that are placed in the product specification. We still do a design of the software architecture, and the result is a set of OOD models and an expanded product specification. We still develop software to a specified design and test the software against specified requirements. The difference is that

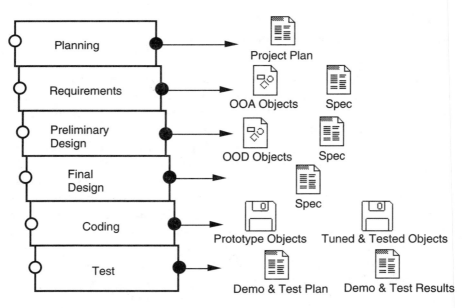

Figure 8.3: Object-oriented lifecycle products

now we do all these things in very small increments; a few objects at a time are specified, developed, and tested.

TO EVOLVE OR NOT TO EVOLVE?

There is one critical decision that will alter the approaches illustrated in Figures 8.2 and 8.3. Will the approved requirements prototype be evolved into the final system, or will it be rewritten entirely in a lower-level language? Many successful prototyping projects involve some code replacement during tuning, but it is usually possible to leverage a majority of the prototype software into production without rewriting it. This is because much of the code for modern systems is in the human-computer interface, and thus does not have difficult performance constraints.

The question to consider here is, what if most or all of the prototype software must be replaced in order to deliver a final product that meets performance needs? What effect would this have on the lifecycle activities and products? The answer depends a lot on when, during the course of the project, it is discovered that there is no way the prototyping environment will be capable of producing a deliverable product. If this is known at the beginning of the project, the requirements activity can be shortened and the coding activity must be lengthened. The requirements effort will be less, because throwaway prototyping will focus mostly on look and feel (including data transformation and presentation), largely ignoring operational issues. Evolutionary prototyping always involves a recognition that the prototyping technology being used will also be the operational technology and that implementation issues should be resolved as they are encountered. Thus the nonevolutionary or throwaway prototype will take less time and effort to iterate as far as it can be without addressing implementation issues. Baseline requirements and design documents can be produced sooner with throwaway prototyping. There may be slightly less overlap, in terms of concurrency, between specification and coding activities.

Yet with throwaway prototyping, the general approach illustrated in Figures 8.2 and 8.3 works well. The names of the phases will stay the same and there can still be a large degree of overlap. The creation of throwaway prototype objects will still be a coding activity; they should be produced and iteratively refined together with the OOA and OOD specifications. The difference is that the tuned and tested prototype object classes will be developed with an entirely different language than the one used to produce the prototype object classes. Obviously, this transition should be anticipated and carefully planned at the beginning of the project. Plan to spend less time in prototype iteration and more time in conventional coding after prototype iteration.

9

Experience

The authors have led, participated in, and provided consulting to dozens of rapid prototyping projects. Most of these projects were not object-oriented, since OORP is a relatively new technique and rapid prototyping, per se, is not. In the early 1980s we used the bundled 4GL and visual programming tools of a high-end relational database management system to develop several management information systems using an evolutionary rapid prototyping approach. Structured analysis and design methods were used concurrently. The prototypes were not thrown away in favor of system rewrites, but evolved over many iterations, all the way through performance testing and tuning, into a final production application. Over a four-year period of experience, many users were pleased with their new applications. Development costs were about half of the costs for conventional development projects.

In the late 1980s we began to apply rapid prototyping to a more diverse set of applications: real-time systems, defense systems, expert systems, engineering, and robotics. Experience was gained using several different kinds of prototyping software on many different development platforms ranging from PCs and workstations to mainframes. The approach was formalized, published, and taught in public seminars domestically in the United States as well as internationally. Now, many organizations continue to use the evolutionary rapid prototyping approach as their standard method of system development.

Having learned what worked well and what didn't from these experiences, the better concepts are carried forward into the new, object-oriented approach. The critical elements for prototyping success will always include:

- careful planning of the prototyping process for each project;
- concurrent use of a formalized methodology for requirements and design specification along with prototype development and iteration;
- focusing on the quickness, rather than completeness, of initial prototype development;
- use of highly productive development tools; and
- allowing for adequate time in the second half of the project for performance testing and tuning.

SMALL OBJECT-ORIENTED BEGINNINGS

Experiments that applied object-oriented analysis and design methods and object-oriented development tools to the rapid prototyping process began in the early 1990s. Two of the earliest experiments were in conjunction with consulting engagements for Laurentian Life Assurance and Xerox Express.

At Laurentian Life, an 800-user point-of-sale support system was under development. Life insurance salesmen were expected to use the system on personal computers in the field. The system performed typical functions such as actuarial lookup and calculation, new policy generation, customizable sales presentations (tailored to the prospect's profile), and remote communication with a mainframe database. The use of an object-oriented rapid prototyping development tool without an object-oriented methodology led the designers to take a hard look at the dichotomy. Observations of the limitations then led to the exploration of OOA/OOD use on subsequent prototyping projects.

A project at Xerox Express involved prototyping a new document search and retrieval system for Xerox PARC research papers. It was one of the first projects on which OOA methods were attempted concurrently with rapid prototype development and iteration. Unfortunately, the project was discontinued due to internal politics before the new system could be implemented, so complete feedback is impossible. However, the introduction of the new methods appeared to have a positive impact and the decision was made to continue in the object-oriented direction.

SEVERAL OBJECT-ORIENTED RAPID PROTOTYPING PROJECTS AT NASA

One of the authors has been the chief methodologist at NASA's Ames Research Center in California, acting as consultant to all software development projects at the center. He has provided training in software engineering as well as on-project methodology and new technology assistance. An approach used with much success is to offer a three-day seminar on object-oriented rapid prototyping, followed by four to eight hours per week consulting on an actual development project staffed by class attendees. Clients work on a rich variety of applications on a diversity of interoperable hardware platforms. There are wind tunnel sensor data acquisition systems, financial information systems, software library management systems, systems that search for extraterrestial intelligence, scientific visualization software, and Internet support tools. These software products run on several varieties of Unix workstations, Macintoshes, Intel™-based PCs, and DEC Vaxes™. Object-oriented rapid prototyping has been used with extraordinary success in all of these environments.

An Object-Oriented Wind Tunnel Sensor Data Acquisition System

This application is a modernization of 400,000 lines of FORTRAN running on a DEC PDP-11™. Sensors attached to the walls of wind tunnels collect data as wind is passed over model experimental aircraft at high speed. The data is then passed through specialized instrumentation to computers under the control of a software application system. There is a user interface that allows test engineers and tunnel operators to set up tests and configure instrumentation and allows researchers to get reports that consist of data reductions.

The project team initially resisted object-oriented rapid prototyping. After several members of the team took a short seminar, they found the approach somewhat attractive. The major appeal stemmed from a lack of confidence in their ability to define user requirements in the conventional manner of specifications based on user interviews. They requested and obtained a somewhat longer workshop on rapid prototyping delivered to the project team on site. At this workshop several project members agreed to try iterative prototyping of a portion of the system—a few of the screens in the user interface.

Most of the project members attended a two-day seminar on rapid prototyping, which was followed by a comprehensive on-site demonstration of an industrial strength prototyping environment. At this point most of the team had been won over by the potential payback of the approach. The author agreed to participate in project planning and design workshops up to eight hours per week. This involvement had a significant impact on decisions that were made regarding the process to be used for software development. Before they even knew what to call their activities, project members were learning and applying OOA, OOD, and C++ programming.

JAM™ from JYAC, Inc. was the prototyping tool. The initial prototype was done on a DOS™-based PC and later ported effortlessly to Unix/Motif. Much sooner than expected, a fully functional prototype taking data from live senors was shown to users and rapid iterations began. After several months of this, one of the NASA managers of the project sought out the author to say how delighted she was with the results produced by the new methods and techniques. As of this writing, the software is mostly written and specified and final integration and acceptance testing is about to begin. Everything is still going very well and users have high confidence in the outcome.

Information Systems for Internet

NASA Science Internet is using OORP to develop several support tools. The scope of the Internet project at NASA has grown to the scale of a small business in order to cope with the demand for connectivity to the "information superhighway" from a seemingly endless supply of new organizations. The project suddenly found itself in a situation where managing its business using manual or semi-automated procedures was no longer feasible. New software applications were needed instantly to combat potentially dire (embarrassing) circumstances. The project staff was not schooled or experienced in the ways of software engineering skills or formal development methods.

Once again, training with followup consulting provided the solution. A short seminar followed by concentrated, hands-on consulting provided a quick start to initiation of a very successful object-oriented rapid prototyping project. Gain Momentum™ for Unix was the prototyping environment for this project. The right methods, excellent tools, and a well-executed formal process caused this experience to be one of the most successful rapid prototyping projects ever for this author.

An On-Orbit Scientific Research System

The following material is based on actual experience but some of the facts have been altered to distance the case study from any actual project. This was unfortunately necessary due to certain procurement sensitivities within NASA at the time of this writing. The authors wish to make it clear that the viewpoints expressed here are not necessarily consistent with the views of the management of NASA, nor do they necessarily accurately represent the factual occurrences on any actual NASA project.

During the contract bidding process for the On-Orbit Scientific Research System (OSRS) OORP was used to develop a detailed dynamic model of desirable software features. The creation of an unambiguous object-oriented analysis model of the specifications provided lessons regarding prototyping tools and techniques. Other educational results include a much better understanding of the software requirements, benefits of rapid prototyping, and differences in managing a rapid prototyping effort versus a traditional one.

The On-Orbit Scientific Research System is intended to be a continuously operating biological laboratory where life science experiments can be performed in space. The unique quality of the facility is the capability to provide simulated gravity levels, from near zero to twice the gravity of Earth. The main components of the facility include habitats, habitat holding units, a centrifuge, and a glovebox. Systems will be controllable from Multi-Purpose Application Consoles (MPAC) on the station along with operations teams and principal investigators on the ground. The contract requires the developer to perform object-oriented rapid prototyping as the technical approach to software development.

Detailed software requirements are to be developed by the contractor, concurrently and iteratively with the design specification efforts. The statement of work instructs the contractor to use a published approach to object-oriented rapid prototyping to prevent use of an ad hoc approach, practiced all too frequently in the name of rapid prototyping. One way to mitigate risk on some NASA contracts is to increase requirements for documentation and formal review. This approach is expensive and has not been proven to reduce risk when specifications are vague, ambiguous, and based on an incomplete understanding of detailed functional software requirements. The specification overkill approach was reversed in creating the software deliverables list for the OSRS project Request for Proposal (RFP). NASA Software Documentation Standards were reduced to a minimal set, consisting mostly of graphic models of the object-oriented analysis and design. The NASA OSRS staff felt that comfort with completeness, correctness, and exactness of a prototype is a better indication of risk reduction than inches of documents produced; and object-oriented requirements and design models are not vague or ambiguous and are much less expensive to produce than conventional narrative prose specifications.

Even after the RFP was issued, some concern remained regarding the applicability of rapid prototyping to this software build. Concerns focused around:

- What is the need? Aren't centrifuge control requirements well known?
- Will it work? Will the contractor know how to do it the right way?
- Aren't appropriate prototyping tools incompatible with the operational environment for the flight software?

Such concerns are normal on many rapid prototyping projects. Rapid prototyping has been used for over a decade, but the purpose, benefits, and techniques of the approach are still not widely understood. Projects that want to pursue rapid prototyping usually need to address concerns about the need, feasibility, and risks involved.

Large lengthy projects, such as OSRS, find themselves continually selling the benefits of the approach to new staff members.

Understanding and appreciation of the productivity and quality benefits of rapid prototyping was broadcast to the OSRS project as the result of an experiment, conducted before contract award, where a primitive prototype was developed and iterated. The tool selected to build the experimental prototype was HyperCard® on the Macintosh, for the following reasons:

- It was easy to learn and easy to use
- It met most of the criteria for a good rapid prototyping tool
- It provided an extremely low-cost solution since it was present on most personal computers in the organization
- All project staff members had access to a Macintosh running HyperCard and thus were able to easily experiment with an AppleShare™ server-based prototype

A preliminary set of graphics-based, object-oriented, analysis and design models was developed in 12 hours. The initial Hyper-Card prototype, consisting of 15 object classes was created in another 8 hours. As is the case with most initial prototypes, it was not totally accepted at the first prototype demonstration with respect to its completeness and exactness. It only served as a quickly built starting point. Figure 9.1 is one of the three pages of the original prototype specification. Over two months the prototype was shown to small groups and individuals in a series of six demonstrations and refinements. Concurrently, the object-oriented graphic models were refined.

The prototype was demonstrated to life science specialists, data acquisition specialists, and ground operations specialists. The requirements that were discovered were in the areas of determining:

- what data researchers would need to have collected about on-board experiments;
- what kinds of sensors would be used to collect the data;
- how data would be displayed on board;
- what data would be transmitted back to the ground;

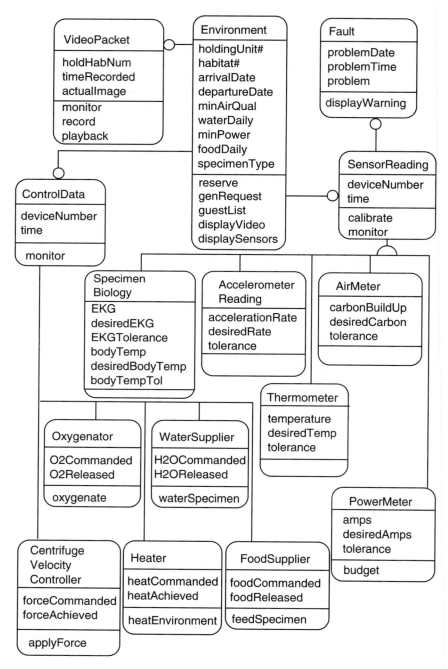

Figure 9.1: Initial OSRS software prototype specification (early prototype object class model)

- how access to data and control functions would be presented to ground-based and on-board users.

The preliminary ideas presented in the initial version of the prototype were rapidly modified, using the HyperCard prototyping tools, based on feedback from project experts. In two months, the prototype was demonstrated and extensively modified six times.

At the end of the summer, the small two-person prototyping team demonstrated the prototype to a well-attended OSRS project all-hands meeting. The demonstration initiated a bit more controversy. It became apparent that different groups within the project (Science, Operations, and Hardware) had divergent views of the strawman in-house design and the detailed software requirements.

Those who had previous experience with rapid prototyping were not surprised at the lack of agreement about detailed software functional requirements. These kinds of internal project debates are much better to have before awarding a contract than at the final acceptance review after the last line of code has been written and tested. The prototypers pointed out that this was one of the main purposes of the technique—to discover lack of agreement on, as well as to establish understanding of, requirements. At this point, most project members agreed there was a critical need for the kind of requirements clarification that rapid prototyping can bring.

A new issue in rapid prototyping is, how much should the human-computer interface look and feel be driven by feedback from prototype reviewers and how much should it be designed using human factors expertise? The basic rule of rapid prototyping is that the users are always right. They get the final say about look, feel, data management, control, and functionality. The problem is that this does not guarantee that users of the delivered software will be forever happy with the look and feel as prototyped. For this type of software, there will be many new sets of users over time. The names and faces of users will change even more rapidly on the OSRS Facility as researchers come and go with new and completed experiments. How can prototype reviewers today guarantee the satisfaction of the users of Centrifuge Facility software in the next decade and beyond?

The approach used during the experiment with rapid prototyping on the Centrifuge project was to allow a human factors expert to build in some of his knowledge of what makes an effective user interface, and then leave those elements in place, unless users objected to them at prototype demonstrations. These considerations included the use of graphical displays along with alphanumeric displays to facilitate readability. Another mechanism used throughout the prototype was the location standardization of certain types of controls. For example, power controls and displays are located in the upper left corner and caution and warning fields are located along the bottom of the screen. Display navigation controls were situated in the screen's lower left section. Emergency controls were placed in the upper right corner. Rectangular buttons were used for display navigation and rounded rectangles were used for other types of controls. Radio buttons were used to select items from mutually exclusive options and checkboxes were used in other cases. The tradeoff between information density and rapidity of perception was an important issue. Packing the most information possible on one screen is useful as it precludes the need to travel around several screens to acquire the required data. However, individual items may take longer to read from a highly packed screen than from one that is more sparsely populated.

Many series of iterations have greatly improved the NASA in-house experimental prototype. The prototype developers have given demonstrations in four different formats: one-on-one, group, project, and private experimentation. Private experimentation is accomplished by making the prototype available on a server, which is accessible to all members on the project.

The initial set of object-oriented specification models was modified concurrently with the prototype software. Figure 9.2 shows the results of the metamorphosis of the object-oriented specification model shown in Figure 9.1 due to prototype iteration.

As expected with a process that allows for incremental versions of a product, new features, added as observations of prototype behavior, lead to the realization of new needs (requirements). Often, the developer is the first to spot a new or improved requirement. On the OSRS project, the developer noted that in most cases, habitats would be grouped in pairs: one habitat would contain the control specimens against which the experimental subjects in the other habitat would be compared. This inspired the creation of the Counterpart button on the habitat display, which is used to open the display for the companion habitat. The juxtaposition of counterpart displays, as

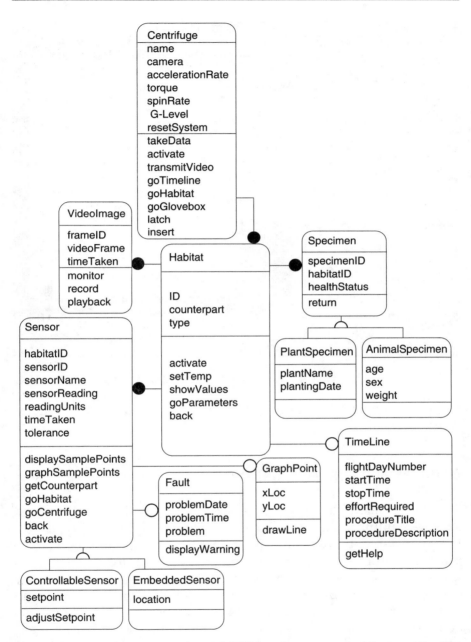

Figure 9.2: Most recent version of OSRS software prototype specification (iterated and refined prototype object model)

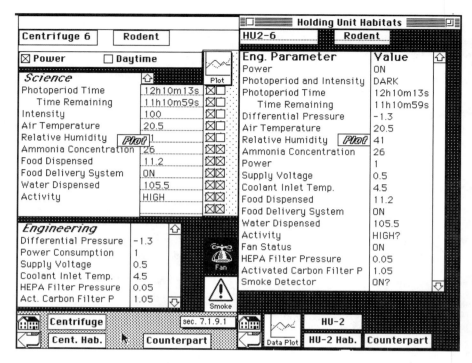

Figure 9.3: Holding unit habitat and Counterpart screens

shown in Figure 9.3, was found to facilitate experimental comparisons and analysis.

A SURVEY-BUILDING APPLICATION[1]

A market research firm, dissatisfied with available automated survey-building tools, decided to develop a rapid prototype of a floppy disk-based interactive questionnaire. The questionnaire, to be bundled with new computer equipment, was to run on both Microsoft Windows and the Macintosh. A purchaser of the new equipment would be asked to insert the floppy disk which would run an application that would ask questions and record answers about the equipment. The survey questions would flow like an interactive electronic novel, tailored dynamically according to the user's responses. The user would then be asked to mail the floppy back to the market research firm where the answers could be collected and analyzed. The application, once ready for market, would be sold to manufacturers of computer equipment to aid them in defining future markets.

Originally, the objective of the project was to provide a proof-of-concept prototype prior to developing the actual survey-builder application. Requirements commissioners hoped that nonprogrammers would be able to use the tool to create individualized questionnaires for many different clients. The developers chose C++, the XVT GUI-portability tool kit (with Windows SDK™, JIT™ Portable Class Library and a graphics library), and the Rumbaugh OMT methodology.

Three major subject areas were developed incrementally: a survey builder, a survey runner, and a disk loader to automate the recovery of results. The survey runner was prototyped first.

Concise object-oriented design resulted in a manageable base upon which many enhancements have been built. The most immediately visible class of design objects are Frames. Each Frame contains one or more Questions, one or more Labels and a decorative Bitmap. Several types of Questions exist, most of which contain one or more Choice objects. Questions may be answered with single selections, multiple selections, text input, and indicators on sliding scales.

The appearance of each screen may be affected by previous answers from the user. Because displayed text may change due to a user's answer, all text is embedded in Label objects. Use of the Label class allowed the implementation of an encapsulated service to alter the wording of the text at runtime if necessary. This concept also allowed the ability to associate Display Logic objects with any Frame, Question, or Choice. In this way, choices of a question that are not applicable to the current user may be hidden.

Flow from screen to screen is managed by Transition Logic services and by grouping collections of Frame instances into Blocks. Special random Blocks are provided to allow a few questions out of many to be chosen and asked. This way, input could be gathered on a wide range of questions without subjecting a single individual to all of the questions.

Since visual appearance is very important, the survey designer can specify multiple columns of choices, multi-line choices, formatted text (font selection, color, bold, underline) and bitmap images. These features turned out to be a challenge when working with XVT.

A first cut Rumbaugh Object Model was developed, then services and attributes were sketched out. The following represents the original thoughts of the designers for some of the object classes.

Class	Services	Attributes
CHOICE	get-selected set-selected get-response set-response is-choice-displayable sel-entry-logic	Value Response Label ID
QUESTION	add-choice-group get-responses get-displayable-choices get-selected is-question-displayable set-entry-logic add-label	Choice Group List Label List ID
FRAME	add-graphics add-table add-question add-layout build-layout activated get displayable questions set entry logic handle events redisplay set editable	GUI-object map Question list Label list Graphics list
BLOCK	add-frame set post frame logic set entry logic activate create displayable frame determine next frame logic	Frame list Entry logic Post frame logic

The first cut was an Instance Model of the Questionnaire and refinements produced the Single Response Instance. OMT uses the instance model to illustrate a test case scenario, showing what the values of the object class attributes are for the actual instances created. Such a model is very useful for object-oriented test planning and is a nice way to plan for prototype demonstrations as well. Jacobson use cases can provide the same capabilities, but are user-oriented rather than application-oriented. Both, however provide scenario models for usage of object classes.

Most of the prototype code has been preserved as the application continues to develop. The second increment, the survey builder, allows the client to design and build questionnaires without writing code or using a compiler. The survey builder creates persistent objects which make up a unique survey. These objects are stored in a data file which can then be read by either the Macintosh or MS Windows version of the survey runner. The builder itself consists of tools for editing questions, laying each out on the screen, and for developing the flow of the questionnaire. Reuse of blocks of questions is also very important and necessitates the capability to cut and paste questions and logic from existing surveys. The initial prototype consisted of one question and was delivered in about a week. The second prototype, delivered about one week later, consisted of one Frame.

The Rumbaugh OMT model was evolved concurrently. The team also used the Class-Responsibility-Collaborator (CRC) cards℠ approach devised by Ward Cunningham and refined by Kent Beck.[2] This approach is based on Rebecca Wirff-Brock's Responsibility-Driven Design methodology and is conceptually very similar to Coad/Yourdon. The main difference is that index cards are used to model objects instead of round-cornered boxes on a graphic model. The information captured is virtually the same.

CRC cards characterize objects along three dimensions: careful choice of *class name* to clarify the understanding of the system; descriptions of *responsibilities* with short phrases and active verbs; helper objects called *collaborators* for understanding of how responsibilities are distributed across a system. The OMT model was reworked and refined using physical index cards until the design seemed well understood by the prototyping team. It was felt that this approach provide a more comprehensive overview of the system than just the OMT model.

A third prototype version, consisting of a functional Question and Frame was ready in about four more days, and about 25 days after the prototype began, Frame and Block sequencing were in place. At that point, the design-developer team split the duties and began to work in parallel. One team member worked on problem domain object classes while the other tackled display object classes.

Early in the prototype development, as the Label object class was developed, the discovery was made that not all object classes have to be uniformly developed. Encapsulation made it possible to develop one portion of the object model at a time while ignoring the others. A new object class, Display Logic, allowed encapsulation of all logic test services (if the message is to "display", then do it this way ...).

The final version of the prototype turned out to be much less of a pilot version demo and much more like the final product than initially planned. The initial contract bid was based on the assumption that the prototype could contain throwaway code that would look good, but would not be used in the final product. Preliminary estimation of the complexity of the project provided little hope of a more long-lived initial product. However, as work began, the emphasis shifted from a throwaway demo to a flexible prototype that could be tailored for specific clients of the market research firm. As the design of the code progressed, emphasis shifted further away from the flexible throwaway prototype idea to real survivable software that was incorporated into the final product. Considerable effort was expended not only to provide the desired functionality, but to anticipate the needs of the final survey builder product. The prototype is the solid foundation on which the survey builder is based, rather than a proof-of-concept demo. Fortunately, new enhancements are being designed around and built upon a solid object-oriented design where encapsulation, polymorphism, and inheritance are at work to allow for expansion without disturbing the existing structure.

TWO ADDITIONAL SMALL PROJECT HIGHLIGHTS

The SoftLib project is reengineering an existing reusable software library management system to have a more user-friendly interface, better search mechanisms, easier access to downloading archived software, support for object-oriented software, and support for specification component reuse. The two most interesting aspects of this project involve multimedia technology and object-oriented productivity metrics. The metrics are discussed in detail in Chapter 10, but it was measured to take 1.08 hours to develop with Gain Momentum, a unit of software that would take 2 hours to develop in C++ and 10 hours in C. Gain Momentum provides support for multimedia data, which is being used in this application to store analysis and design models as viewable high-resolution images.

Finally, another interesting project illustrates that sometimes the rules can be bent and brilliant success still achieved. A young C programmer, J. R. Gloudemans, took a seminar in object-oriented rapid prototyping from one of the authors. A copy of Coad and Nicola's *Object-Oriented Programming*,[3] containing four application examples implemented in both Smalltalk and C++ was provided to the students. J. R. was asked by three researchers to create an application that would allow them to develop computer-generated three-dimensional wire-frame models of experimental aircraft and generate geometry files that could be input to computational fluid dynamics analytical software that would study the designs for potential flaws. J. R. started with some of the C++ object classes contained on the floppy disk included with the OOP book and modified them to make floating tool pallettes with geometry sliders that would allow the researchers to dynamically alter the various components of aircraft geometry: wing, fuselage, tail, and so forth. Operating on a shoe-string budget, he found a public domain application called Forms that would provide a graphic user interface with Motif-style widgets using code-free visual programming. He found it was easy to invoke the C++ object class services using Forms button widgets and to access the object class attributes using Forms field widgets.

He built a very small initial prototype consisting of just a handful of object classes and showed it to the potential users within a week of when they made their initial request. They were not really impressed with what they saw, but recognized that it was ready quickly and that it had potential. They gave him a list of requested additions and refinements to see how he would handle the changes. J. R.'s C++ classes were well encapsulated and loosely coupled within the application. He also made very effective use of inheritance. As a result, it was easy for him to make requested additions and modifications without having to rewrite very much of the prototype.

Two or three times a week, the researchers would descend on J. R., view the current prototype version and request changes and additions. This went on for three months, at the end of which time the users were sufficiently satisfied with the application to start using it for real work. They are still using it, months later, and still making frequent requests for refinements. The application now has a nice, crisp, productive feel to it and a user interface beautiful enough to take one's breath away.

But the most remarkable part about J. R.'s story is not that he was able to make three fussy users happy; it is rather that he did so in three months. His three-month-old 30-object class application provides very similar functional capabilities to another application created previously for a different user group at the same organization. The other application required a team of six people three years to create what J. R. built in three months!

But, remember that we said J. R. bent the rules? He did no specifications and put the application into production without tuning. Did he just get lucky, or is such a process repeatable? From looking at his well-crafted object classes, we believe he carries an elegant object-oriented design around in his head. Using compiled C++ and real data, he was doing tuning as he went along, addressing user performance issues as they surfaced. The crisp response of geometry shape changes to user control operation was always a critical interface consideration. For a small application (30-object classes), with few users (three), and a single developer, this seat-of-the-pants approach will probably produce acceptable results most of the time. So, the sky does not always fall when developers do not create formal OOA/OOD models and neglect formal stress tests. We still maintain, however, that J. R. would not have been slowed down by OOA/OOD modeling (it would have made his modifications even easier) and stress-testing his objects just before releasing the application for production use would have reduced risk of sudden performance failure.

ENDNOTES

1. Reynolds, J., and Lasby, J., "Dealing with Shared Persistent Objects," *Object Magazine*, 4(2), May 1994, pp. 51–52.

2. Beck, K., "Think Like An Object," *Unix Review, 9* (10), pp. 39–43.

3. Coad, P., and Nicola, J., *Object-Oriented Programming*, New York: Yourdon Press (Prentice-Hall), 1993.

10

Projects

The following material is not intended for managers. True, it is about how to effectively control an object-oriented rapid prototyping project. The management of OORP should not be left to those who have management job titles, however. Such projects are in too much of a hurry to be closely controlled by hierarchies of management in traditional roles. An effective rapid prototyping team is a small, largely self-managing team, where leadership roles are those of facilitator, coordinator, and technical leader, rather than manager. Those who participate in object-oriented rapid prototyping projects are the ones who get to apply the following principles and practices—regardless of job title. The role of others, with official management job titles, is to facilitate and not interfere. Of course, there can be a manager who is also the technical leader or facilitator for one or more activities on an OORP project. In that case, it will be necessary for the manager to be able to put his or her management hat on and take it off at will.

SKILLS NEEDED FOR OBJECT-ORIENTED RAPID PROTOTYPING

Team building is an absolute necessity. The project participants will want to take an active role in selecting teammates. Team members need to consider what skills they can contribute and what skills are expected from colleagues in order to arrive at the proper skill mix. Figure 10.1 is a matrix showing the required OORP activities and skills required to perform those activities.

	ANALYST	DESIGNER	DBA	DEVELOPER	REVIEWER
SERVICE MODELING	●	●		●	●
INFORMATION MODELING	●	●	●	●	●
CONTROL MODELING	●	●		●	●
DMS			●	●	
PROTOTYPING				●	●
WALKTHROUGHS					●

Figure 10.1: Skill matrix for object-oriented rapid prototyping

Each person on the team must have an understanding of the changes required to the development lifecycle. Everyone should contribute to the project plan. If it is the first OORP project, it will take longer than subsequent ones, because the project team will experience a learning curve and because libraries for future reuse are being built. Each subsequent project in an application domain will consume shorter and shorter periods of time.

The team must be able to agree on the assignment of project roles, such as class librarian, object modeler, prototyper, reusable component-builder, database architect, and reuse researcher. The researcher should begin immediately after project kick-off to see if any useful class libraries exist in the public domain or from a vendor.

The team should invest in a class repository management system early in the project. It is helpful to have a convenient storage facility for the objects that have been tested through prototyping so they will be easily available to all developers for the remainder of the project. Hopefully, the class repository manager will not only provide housing for reusable objects, but will serve traditional configuration management functions as well. Because of the number of iterations that might be expected, a log of versions of prototypes and changes incorporated between versions provides a rich source of data for a measurement system.

Since rapid prototyping is concurrent engineering, all skills are needed from the beginning of the project to the end. After the team has formed itself, it needs to evaluate individual potential contributions carefully, making sure there are no critical skills missing. If it is not possible to recruit the necessary talent, then training needs must be identified.

Project teams need to market OORP continuously across the entire organization. Advertise successful outcomes. Publish testimonials from happy requirements commissioners. Get everyone using OORP. If acceptance is restricted to isolated *islands of excellence*, the benefits of reusable object class libraries will be severely limited.

Early sets of object classes will not, and should not, be acceptable to requirements commissioners: multiple iterations and incremental building of the set of object classes is the norm. Dissatisfaction with the early version of the prototype should not demotivate the team but have the opposite effect. Team members should always keep in mind that avoiding the risk of delivering an unsatisfactory final product is the reason for rapid prototyping and that means iteration.

A newly formed team might consider jump-starting their project by contracting with OORP consultants and trainers. This type of expert help is appropriate with the institutionalization of any new technology.

Lastly, the powerful *not-invented-here* syndrome seems present within everyone to some degree, and must be fought with a new cultural attitude. In order for teamwork to succeed, reuse is the key to highly leveraged productivity.

RESOURCES FOR THE DEVELOPMENT ENVIRONMENT

Chapter 4 described the types of tools needed for OORP development and how to evaluate the various products against the most critical criteria. Don't forget that other software will be needed in support of the prototyping tools. A good compiler for an object-oriented language such as C++ will be necessary, a data management system if the prototyping tool does not have one, a word processor, a computer-aided drawing tool, analysis and design CASE tools (discussed at length in the next chapter), a class library management tool, a configuration management tool, and a desktop publishing package.

The best examples of useful products in these support software categories are written for Unix, Microsoft Windows, and Macintosh. This implies that each of the team members should have at least one personal workstation running at least one of these operating systems, even if development is targeted toward a large multi-user computer. If anyone out there still has a dumb terminal on his or her desk, send it to the surplus equipment warehouse immediately!

MEASURING AND CONTROLLING OORP PRODUCTIVITY

How can the team know how well it is doing in terms of quality and productivity if no measurements of those elements have been established? During the planning stages, how can a project team know when major milestones will occur, when the software will be ready to deliver, and whether the software and its data will fit on the target hardware platforms?

The software engineering field has been searching for decades for a way to definitively size software. Precise sizing provides a means for determining, accurately, the answers to the following questions:

- How much will it cost to develop a proposed new software application?
- How well will the software fit within the target computer's available storage and memory?
- How are individual programmers performing in terms of units of software produced per unit of project time elapsed?
- When will the work in progress be ready for use?

Good metrics would make new application cost/benefit analyses lead to correct decisions more frequently. There would be less processing of expensive change requests during system development to reconfigure baseline hardware architectures as true software size becomes apparent. Quality initiatives could make use of better process improvement metrics. Project management, with good metrics, would be more effective.

Most software engineering metrics are heuristics based on experience. Another widely used metric is the source line of code (SLOC); developers guess how many SLOCs will be in the final product, and then multiply the error of this estimate by errors in the estimate of how many lines of code can be produced in one person hour. Less widely used is Function Point Analysis[1,2]—a measure of software size that is language independent and has a more precise definition than the SLOC.

Many software engineers are resistant to the collection of metrics. They feel they are too busy, don't know what's in it for them, have no idea what happens to the data they supply, and fear the metrics will be used to judge them unfavorably. Organizational structure and culture affect the possibility of success. The benefits of metrics can and should be explained to project team members. Without an accurate effort reporting system based on a truthful work breakdown structure (WBS), projects have no hope for realistic in-process measurements. And without such measurements, it is impossible to know, before the end of a project when it is expensive to correct, whether or not the project is on the targeted course.

Management may foster the fear of metrics by complaining about the numbers when they are revealed. It is often a good idea to keep the metrics separated from identification of individual developers. Time must be allowed for reporting the input necessary to metrics: effort, errors found in reviews, and others. Allowance must be made for the extra overhead of collecting, synthesizing, analyzing, graphing, and reporting metrics.

Reuse Metrics

We've known for some time that the type and amount of reuse will have a positive effect on productivity and estimates of productivity. In Barry Boehm's 1981 classic work, *Software Engineering Economics*,[3] he suggested an Adaptation Adjustment Factor (AAF) to account for the reuse effect. This factor is integrated into most automated versions of his COCOMO (COnstructive COst MOdel) model. There are two steps in estimating with reuse using COCOMO:

Step 1 is to calculate the AAF multiplier from the following equation:

$$AAF = DT*DM + MT*CM + IT*IM$$

where

DT = Percentage of time typically spent in design

DM = Percentage of design modification required to reuse the existing program module

MT = Percentage of time spent in modification

CM = Percentage of code modification required to reuse the existing program module

IT = Percentage of time spent in integration

IM = Percentage of reintegration for the existing program module.

Step 2 is to compute an equivalent size:

S(equiv) = S * AAF / 100

where

S(equiv) = Equivalent size

S = Total size

AAF = Adaptation Adjustment Factor

Modernization of these ideas to include OORP would require a unit of size other than source lines of code (SLOC), and most likely, the adjustment to include more phases than just design, modification, and reintegration. In addition, these phases would require a percentage of total development time to replace the MT, IT, and IM. Reusable object classes are one of the major benefits of OORP. When object-oriented specification methods are employed in the creation of the prototype, then analysis and design models may be reused as well, increasing savings. Therefore, further modernization to the COCOMO formula would suggest that *program module* be replaced with *object class, analysis model, design model*, or any other appropriate deliverable.

Almost all object-oriented practitioners claim reuse as one of the major returns on the object-oriented investment. However, the actual amount of savings and exactly how much of the system is reused are often unknown. In addition, it is rarely known whether the reuse is pure (unchanged items) and how much is derived or modified (Fig. 10.2).

If source code is the item being reused, there is often a need to rewrite or update the reused specification document, update the reused design document, recompile and check the compiled source code, and verify that the source code, was not contaminated during the transport.

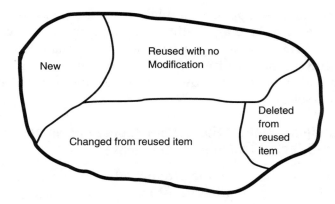

Figure. 10.2: Graphic illustration of system reuse

It is useful to construct an object-oriented system reuse profile whose characteristics could include:

- Percentage of object classes and services imported from an existing library outside this system
- Percentage of object classes and services imported from an existing library for this system
- Percentage of reused object classes and services used without modification
- Percentage of reused object classes and services used with modification

Reuse has costs that may be hidden, such as the cost of the library or repository where reusable articles are stored. The cost of communicating the contents of the repository is not expense-free, especially in large organizations. Bell Labs discovered, when promoting their reuse program, that there must be both a thief and a victim to make reuse plausible. The thief must be cunning enough to sniff out what is available and does not need to be reinvented. The victim must be clever enough to produce a product worthy of reuse. The victim must find a way to advertise the existence and quality of the product and the thief must not suffer from the NIH (Not Invented Here) syndrome. The NIH syndrome causes some developers to consistently apply their creative juices to developing new object classes instead of starting with existing ones and adapting them to the new application when possible. Reuse is doubtless an excellent way to leverage both quality and productivity, but just believing that it is a worthy goal will not be adequate to ensure the proper return on the investment. Only the proper metrics will prove that when additional effort is devoted to reusable components there is a distinct payoff.

Conventional Metrics Discourage Rapid Prototyping, Object-Oriented Techniques, and Reuse

The only way to know the productivity rate in your specific environment is to conduct project post mortems and make certain that actuals are accurately collected. But some metrics for measuring effort, such as lines of code, are worse than none for object-oriented rapid prototyping. Software developers are paid to develop software applications, not to write lines of code.

Suppose that two developers are working on the same application in different organizations. One is using a third generation language (3GL), such as FORTRAN, and another using a fourth generation language (4GL). The 4GL developer will have fewer lines of code than the 3GL developer (perhaps by an order of magnitude) for the same amount of functionality. This is documented by many studies and is well presented in Dreger's *Function Point Analysis.*[4]

This fact is complicated by several arguments. Some argue that 4GL code is not as efficient or robust as 3GL. Others say that, although the 4GL programmer writes fewer lines of code, he or she is done sooner, so the metrics work out satisfactorily. Finally, some advocate collecting SLOC metrics that are language specific, thus compensating for differences.

It is not necessary to argue over the goodness of 4GL versus 3GL. Do you believe that third generation languages were a significant productivity improvement over second generation languages such as Assembler and Autocoder? Wasn't Assembler a big improvement over raw machine language? Isn't there a noticeable trend here in terms of number of lines of code needed to produce a given amount of functionality? The history of programming environment development has always been to create new languages that increase programmer productivity by requiring *fewer lines of code* to produce a given amount of functionality. If a metrics system rewards programmers based on how many lines of code they write per hour, it will constitute a bad incentive (rewarding productivity degradation).

While it is true that 4GL programmers will finish coding a given amount of functionality sooner than their 3GL programmer counterparts, this does not mean that they will finish a similar development project significantly faster. The reason this is true is that they will not write requirements and design specifications or test plans any faster. Suppose that coding is 20 percent of total development effort. Then, suppose that a 4GL programmer can do the coding in 10 percent the time required for a 3GL programmer. This will result in a total 18 percent productivity improvement—not very dramatic. On the other hand, the 4GL programmer will probably write 10 percent of the number of lines of code needed by the 3GL programmer. Therefore, a SLOC metrics system will show that a 4GL programmer is very unproductive, compared to a 3GL programmer—unless the organization has been collecting 4GL metrics previously and never attempts to compare productivity between environments. The bottom line is that, even if you collect 4GL metrics, there are always vendors developing new higher productivity languages and development systems. Consider how badly SLOC systems fail in visual programming environments where icons, menu choices, and drawing tools take the place of text-based syntax.

Complexity Metrics

In order to understand productivity, it is necessary to understand complexity. An average object-oriented developer may be able to produce and implement an average of n objects in one week. However, there are factors (Jones calls them *environmental factors*; Boehm calls them *cost drivers*) that can make a particular object class take extremely different amounts of implementation time, even in the same language, than the average object class. How much data is to be managed? How many services does the object provide? How much work do the services do? What external interfaces does the object class have? We need new approaches to determine the relative difficulty of implementing object classes so that effort and schedule estimations will be accurate.

Some useful metrics may be borrowed from traditional programming techniques to measure overall complexity and quality.

They involve the concepts of coupling, cohesion, scope, leveling, relationships, information hiding, and decisions.

In traditional procedural/relational systems:

Coupling means the number of interfaces between modules and the amount of data passed between them. Low coupling, or few interfaces is encouraged.

Cohesion means how well a module performs one and only one function. High cohesion, or modules performing one and only one function, is encouraged. The practice localizes problems and changes and improves maintainability. Lack of cohesion, or a module that performs multiple functions, is indicative of one that should probably be split into two or more modules.

Scope refers to scope of control or scope of effect. Rules of thumb for the optimum number of items under the control of another have developed.

Levels refers to levels of decomposition. Many levels indicate a complex application.

Relationships are connections between informational entities, or collections of pieces of data.

Information hiding is placing the information directly with the cohesive function as opposed to passing it around levels of a control structure with opportunities of corruption. It has been encouraged for many years.

Decision complexity is measured in various ways, such as numbers of levels of nested decisions coded in a programming language or pseudo code. A time-tested measure of decision complexity is the McCabe metric.[5]

Interpretations of some of these definitions become slightly modified with object orientation:

Coupling is when one object uses services or attributes of another. Reduction of coupling between objects improves encapsulation. As with procedural design, the larger the number of couples, the greater the degree of interdependence and difficulty of maintenance, and the lower the potential for reuse.

Cohesion of services refers to similarity of methods within an object. High degrees of similarity leads to high degrees of encapsulation. Low cohesion indicates that two or more object classes may be more appropriate than just one.

Scope represents the number of items belonging to another or controlled by another. In object technology the number of derived classes of a base class could represent scope (degree of specialization).

Levels in object-oriented technology refer to the depth of the inheritance tree. Levels represent the impact of the properties of the ancestor. Ancestors with large numbers of services can have great impact of descendants who inherit those services.

Function Point Metrics

Function Point Analysis (FPA) requires the estimation of how many Inputs, Outputs, Inquiries, Files, and Interfaces a proposed system will contain. An *Input* is an item of data sent by the user to the software system for processing, often to add, change or delete something. An *Output* is an item of information processed by the software system for the end user. Only unique inputs and outputs are counted; uniqueness requires a different format and different processing logic. An *Inquiry* is a direct inquiry into a data structure (database or file) to search for specific data, but performing no update functions. A *File* is the repository of data stored for an application. An *Interface* refers to data stored external to the system (another application, user, device), but used by the system under consideration.

Both Dreger and Jones present schemes for further identifying and counting each of these elements and for assigning a complexity weighting to them. They also present tables for converting function points to lines of code for various languages. The beauty of this approach is that it is language independent; the same number of function points will be developed, based on the analysis of the proposed system, regardless of the language that will be chosen for implementation. Conventional structured analysis and design (SA/SD) methodologies produce specifications from which function point estimates can be extracted in a manner that, while not always precisely repeatable, is typically more accurate than a SLOC-based estimate.

Jones suggests adjusting the raw function point count (identified, classified, weighted function points) to account for environmental factors that may be expected to affect the overall development process. These environmental factors (e.g., the requirement that data and or process be distributed) may also be weighted to correspond to the degree of system influence expected (e.g., if data must be distributed among several platforms, the weighting for this environmental factor might be a 3 or 4 on a scale of 1 to 5). Jones recommends the consideration of 14 specific environmental factors, reminiscent of Boehm's COCOMO cost drivers. Like Boehm, Jones also recommends understanding the environment well enough to modify the factors to modernize them when necessary and thereby calibrate the model. Following the computation of function points adjusted for environmental factors, they may optionally be converted to lines of code.

Unfortunately, the very reason for the success of FPA is also its major weakness. Since structured specifications must be fairly complete before a meaningful estimate can be generated (how else can you possibly know how many queries and files will be required?), FPA does not work well when a rapid prototyping approach is used. The prototyper needs a reliable estimate in order to plan for completion of prototype iteration, yet cannot completely prespecify requirements. Requirements discovery is one of the results of the rapid prototyping effort.

Also, it is not clear that the counting philosophy of FPA is compatible with the OORP development technique. The concept of a *program* with inputs, outputs, and queries no longer works, nor does the concept of a *file*, since, in the object-oriented paradigm, an object encapsulates both data and services. Even though, in the ultimate implementation, services will be realized in programmed code and data will be realized in some sort of data structure, those details are not available at an early stage of the project for rapid prototyping.

Object-Oriented Productivity Metrics (OOPM)

What is required is something new—object-oriented productivity metrics (OOPM). OOPM is derived from Function Point Analysis. Metrics for file complexity are translated into metrics for the attribute complexity of an object. Metrics for program complexity are translated into the encapsulated service complexity of an object. External interface complexity is counted in much the same way. Like FPA, OOPM is language-independent, but it is also compatible with object-oriented analysis and rapid prototyping. The developer will count object-oriented effort points (OOEPs) instead of Function Points. An OOEP is a unit of measure used to determine the complexity of an object-oriented software application.

Estimating the development of an object class requires knowledge of the object's data (attributes) and services, as well as what data will be shipped from and to external entities. These data can be captured from the brief, preliminary rapid analysis done prior to development of the initial prototype.

Beginning with the encapsulated data, a simple object is defined as one with fewer than seven attributes; an average object has seven to 14 attributes; and complex objects have more than 14 attributes. Project experience has shown that most of the time spent developing the data structure of an object class is spent in requirements analysis and design. Actual development of data structures takes little time once the design details have been specified. In addition, *simple, average,* and *complex* are defined in terms of object-oriented effort points (OOEPs). A simple object is 3 OOEPs, an average object is 5 OOEPs, and a complex object is 8 OOEPs.

Services, or methods, considered separately, are categorized using ideas from both Dreger and Coad/Yourdon. Four categories are add/modify/delete services, system screen (menus, helps) services, output services, and computationally intensive services. They are weighted for complexity based on the amount of data processed. Add/modify/delete services are 3 OOEPs, 4 OOEPs or 6 OOEPs depending on whether the object class attribute structure is simple, average, or complex. System screen services get a modest 4 OOEP weight since the processing of data is minimal. Computationally intensive services will always require more effort, so a flat 8 OOEP weight makes sense.

Finally, as with FPA, interfaces to external entities must be considered since they will add to the amount of effort required to develop the system. Again, simple, average, and complex weightings are a good place to start. When an external entity interfaces with only one object class, it is considered simple, with an OOEP weight of 7; an external entity that interfaces with two to five object classes is average and gets 10 OOEP points; an external entity that interfaces with more than 5 object classes is complex and gets 15 OOEPs.

All of the OOEP complexity counts above are directly derivable from similar function point counts. The object-oriented metrics are summarized in the matrix shown in Figure 10.3, which summarizes the system for counting OOEPs.

Counting Object-Oriented Effort Points (OOEPs)

Before any estimate may be prepared, a high-level specification of system requirements must be prepared. These preliminary requirements will define preliminary object classes, an initial set of at-

	Simple	Average	Complex
Object	**< 7 Attributes**	**7-14 Attributes**	**> 14 Attributes**
	3 OOEPs	**5 OOEPs**	**8 OOEPs**
Service:			
Add, Modify, Delete	3 OOEPs	4 OOEPs	6 OOEPs
Output	4 OOEPs	5 OOEPs	7 OOEPs
System Screen	4 OOEPs	N/A	N/A
Computation	N/A	N/A	8 OOEPs
External Entity	**< 3 Objects**	**3-5 Objects**	**> 5 Objects**
	7 OOEPs	**10 OOEPs**	**15 OOEPs**

Figure 10.3: Matrix for determining object-oriented effort points

tributes and services, and external entity interfaces. For a prototyping project, these models are intentionally incomplete. Estimates should allow for an expansion factor to obtain a total development effort estimate. Every day that passes on a development project provides more insight and project knowledge; estimates that are revised frequently become more and more accurate.

A tutorial example will demonstrate how to apply OOPM to rapid OOA. Returning to the Harbor Information System (please refer back to Figures 5.3, 5.4, and 5.5 for the following example), we can set up a worksheet to begin to determine OOEPs for this example. Figure 10.3 describes the following counting procedure. There are ten simple object classes in the Harbor Information System, for an OOEP count of 30; six simple add/modify/delete services for 18 OOEPs, 5 simple output services for 20 points, one computation (calcRent) for 8 points and, let's say one menu and one help screen, for 8 more points. This gives a total of 84 OOEPs for object attributes and services. Referencing the Harbor Information System source/ sink diagram, there are five external entities. Harbor Manager and Employee are of average complexity and get 10 points each. Acme Placement Agency Database, Ship Owner, and Payless Shoes are

41. This brings the grand total for the Harbor Information System to 125 OOEPs.

Converting OOEPs to Hours

Dreger states that it takes about 20 hours to code one function point in a third generation language such as COBOL. Examples of other languages in this range are Pascal, JOVIAL, FORTRAN, ALGOL, and C (C is identified as the least productive language in this list). Object-oriented software development projects typically use languages such as C++ or Smalltalk. Dreger's data indicates that object-oriented programming languages (OOPLs) require about one-fifth as many lines of code per function point as a third generation language, due presumably, to language extensibility and component reuse through inheritance. This puts OOPLs in almost the same category as a 4GL. If it takes 20 hours per function point in a 3GL, it probably takes about four hours per function point in an object-oriented language such as C++ or Smalltalk.

Multiplying the count of OOEPs by four hours per OOEP leads to a conclusion that the Harbor Information System example could be developed in 500 person hours (4 hours x 125 OOEPs) or roughly three person months. This estimate includes OOA, OOD, code construction with an OOPL, test and all documentation, bearing in mind that documentation effort is quite variable, depending on an organization's standards.

Object-Oriented Quality Metrics

Project teams could be provided recognition and rewards according to their proficiency in rapid development of new object classes. An object class is something of greater perceived value to application users than lines of code or function points. Developers may also be rewarded for reusing object classes. This could be accomplished by simply not subtracting anticipated reuse from initial OOEP counts. Then reuse would be a developer's option for increasing perceived productivity.

OOPM provides a way to create reliable sizing and effort estimates very early in the life of a project—before requirements have been finalized—based on preliminary object-oriented graphics models. Using a rapid prototyping approach, OOPM will provide an estimate of how long it will take to develop the initial prototype and an expansion ratio can be used to estimate how long it will take to develop the entire application. The same expansion ratio can also be used to estimate how many objects will exist in the final application.

Metrics have been collected by the authors on a few projects. The metrics are kept on time and effort required for object class development, using the development environments shown in Figure 4.1. Four years of data have been averaged, showing that four hours per OOEP is about right. To achieve accurate metrics in your environment, it will be necessary to calibrate the model using historical data collected in your environment over a period of time.

ENDNOTES

1. Jones, C., *Programming Productivity*, New York: McGraw-Hill, Inc., 1986.
2. Jones, C., *Applied Software Measurement: Assuring Productivity and Quality*, New York: McGraw-Hill, Inc., 1991.
3. Boehm, B., *Software Engineering Economics*, Englewood Cliffs, NJ: Prentice-Hall, Inc., 1981.
4. Dreger, J. B., *Function Point Analysis*, Englewood Cliffs, NJ: Prentice-Hall, Inc., 1989.
5. McCabe, T., and Butler C., "Design Complexity Measurement and Testing," *Communications of the ACM*, 32(12), December, 1989, 1415–1425.

RECOMMENDED READINGS

Basili, V. R., "Software Modeling and Measurement: The Goal/Question/ Metric Paradigm," white paper, University of Maryland Institute for Advanced Computer Studies, Department of Computer Science.

Bieman, J. M., "Deriving Measures of Software Reuse in Object Oriented Systems," Technical Report #CS-91–112, NATO Collaborative Research Grants Program, 1991.

Chidamber, S. R. and Kemerer, C. F., "Towards a Metrics Suite for Object Oriented Design," *Proceedings of OOPSLA '91*, pp. 197–211.

Fairley, R., "Risk Management for Software Projects," *IEEE Software*, 11(3), May, 1994, 57–67.

Grady, R. B., *Practical Software Metrics for Project Management and Process Improvement*, Englewood Cliffs, NJ: Prentice-Hall, Inc., 1992.

Grady, R. B., and Caswell, D. R., *Software Metrics: Establishing a Company-Wide Program*, Englewood Cliffs, NJ: Prentice-Hall, Inc., 1987.

Harmon, P., and Taylor, D. A., *Objects in Action: Commercial Applications of Object-Oriented Technologies,* Reading, MA: Addison-Wesley, 1993.

Londeix, B., *Cost Estimation for Software Development,* Reading, MA: Addison-Wesley, 1987.

Loomis, M. E. S., "Distributed Object Databases," *JOOP,* March-April, 1993.

Putnam, L. H., "The Economic Value of Moving up the SEI Scale," McLean, VA: Quantitative Software Management, Inc., 1993.

Putnam, L. H., and Myers, W., *Measures for Excellence: Reliable Software, On Time, Within Budget,* New York: Prentice-Hall, Inc., 1992.

Rodriguez, V., and Tsai, W. T., "A Tool for Discriminant Analysis and Classification of Software Metrics," *Information and Software Technology, 29*(3), April, 1987, 137–150.

11

Computer-Aided Software Engineering (CASE)

Almost everyone agrees that Computer-Aided Software Engineering (CASE) tools were oversold in the 1980s, paving the way for the age of disillusionment in the 1990s. In the late 1980s, we noted that one large aerospace firm bought 80 CASE Unix workstation seats, costing about $50,000 each, for a 300-person project. The CASE product was one of the very best real-time structured analysis and design support tools. A year later, after an initial frenzy of mousing and clicking and dragging and dropping, most of the workstations were sitting in storage unused and not one page of acceptable requirements documentation had been produced.

Other projects at the same aerospace firm used this same CASE tool to produce a documented 50 percent savings in effort required to produce specifications compared to similar efforts without CASE tools. We conclude that the difference was due to flaws in the application of the CASE tool on the large project that failed, not flaws in the CASE tool itself. Wags were overheard joking that, "A fool with a tool will only do more foolish things faster."

There was little or no requirements analysis or design methodology training offered to the people who occupied the 80 seats referenced above. A short three-day course was provided by the vendor, and primarily covered how to use the powerful but complex tool. What was missing was a thorough understanding of Paul Ward and Steve Mellor's methodology upon which the product was based. The attitude was that since so much money had been spent on CASE workstations, the requirements definition process must be fully automated now and the workstations could be operated by low-skilled *requirements clerks*. Many of the CASE operators were new hires fresh out of college.

The preceding story is an illustration of how, sometimes, people have been seduced into thinking they are going to get more out of a CASE tool than is possible. In attempting the impossible, they produce disastrous results. The original idea behind CASE tools was to spare systems analysts and software designers from spending their valuable time in drafting activities by providing them with software that automates the production of graphically oriented analysis and design methodology deliverables. If solving that critical problem is kept in sight, and the continuing need to have highly skilled, well-trained analysts and designers is recognized, use of CASE tools can produce significant productivity improvements.

THE ROLE OF CASE TOOLS IN OBJECT-ORIENTED RAPID PROTOTYPING

Any software that supports the software engineering process in any way can technically be considered a CASE tool. This can include debuggers, test support, language-sensitive editors, and many other programming-oriented tools. These are often referred to as "lower CASE" tools because they are used toward the end of the lifecycle, and the tools that support analysis and design are sometimes called "upper CASE." For rapid prototyping, we are primarily interested in the upper CASE tools.

For upper CASE tools, one of the big selling points is the ability to check the developer's specifications against the rules of the methodology in use. This is called *consistency checking*. Object-oriented analysis and design methods have fewer rules than structured analysis and design (SA/SD). Simplification is primarily due to the absence of elaborate functional and data hierarchies and decomposition, and to the absence of format switching between analysis (data flow diagrams) and design (structure charts). Using SA/SD, one moves from data flow diagrams, control flow diagrams, and entity relationship diagrams into architecture diagrams and finally to structure charts through transformation and transaction analysis. Hierarchical decomposition causes many problems with partitioning, balancing, leveling, and conservation; there are complicated structured rules for these elements of a structured specification. Without hierarchical decomposition, there is much less need for consistency checking.

Object-oriented CASE tools need to do less and should therefore cost less than structured CASE tools. The object-oriented products are primarily drawing tools, explaining much of the decrease in price. Drawing tools that are just drawing tools with no built-in object-oriented constructs cost even less. Drawing is at least 80 percent of what most users do with a CASE tool. For some CASE tools, however, drawing is their weakest feature. This leads to the conclusion that selection of simple drawing software instead of a CASE tool to support OOA and OOD is often the right decision.

In the area of prototyping, some high-end CASE products have the ability to generate a software "prototype." In some instances, the prototype generated is of fairly impressive quality. When this happens, there is a positive and strong coupling between the software and the specification. Warning to the reader: Don't be seduced! A well-constructed drawing can appear to be a good design when, in fact, it may bear little relationship to the real user requirements and may actually represent a poor design. The "if it was produced on a computer, it must be right" syndrome applies also to CASE tools—attractive drawings make impressive presentation materials, but may or may not be adequate as an application design.

A prototype that is easy to iterate cannot be generated by a CASE tool unless there is a means of debugging at the drawing stage. To put it another way, when the requirements commissioners see the prototype and want changes, what will be changed—the software or the drawing? If the software is changed, it will quickly lose all coupling with the drawing. Is the prototype generated in a language that is easy to modify (many products generate C or C++)? If changes will always occur in the drawing, there should be consideration given to whether or not the drawing tools provide an environment suitable for debugging thorny software problems. At present, we know of no CASE tool vendors who recognize this problem, much less provide a good solution. They are often too busy selling code generators.

When requirements commissioners request changes to the prototype, the temptation is to skip the object-oriented CASE tool and go directly to the prototype software, which is easy to access and change. Developers find instant gratification in viewing the results.

It often appears that placing the CASE models between the requested changes and the prototype is time-consuming and unnecessary. This is a dangerous situation because it will tempt prototypers to skimp on the models and only change the prototype after obtaining feedback from requirements commissioners. Iterations that skip updates to the models and go directly to the prototype can appear to be quicker at first, but the short-term productivity gains cannot last, since complex changes will be much more difficult without a good overall system roadmap. When the prototype gets too far ahead of the models, trying to reverse-engineer the specs out of the prototype becomes an arduous and sometimes impossible task.

Of course, there are products that help leverage productivity and some good reasons for using them to support OORP. A simple drawing tool does not provide enough leverage to make changes easy. A good OOA/OOD CASE tool has enough intelligence about the methodology being used that it does much of the work for the specifier and supports changes in a methodology-smart way. Graphic objects that should be connected stay connected. References to attributes in service specs might be automatically updated when the attributes are modified. The service specs, attribute definitions, and graphic models are all easy to transfer to a word processing document when it is time to create a deliverable specification. Features like these will make even the most senior developer appreciate the value of using such a tool concurrently while prototyping—as long as it doesn't cost too much and is a good drawing tool as well.

CASE tools offer the promise, if not the total fulfillment, of support for every activity of object-oriented rapid prototyping. A CASE tool could support integrated project management by automating the object-oriented productivity metrics discussed in Chapter 10. Support for rapid analysis takes the form of supporting the creation of the initial OOA models. When it is time to develop the initial prototype, the CASE-based models can be printed out and provide a blueprint to guide the developer. It is during prototype iteration that a good CASE tool will provide the biggest payoff, making it possible to make the specification changes as fast as the prototyper can make changes to the software. Before tuning, during the final design activity, consistency checks against OOA and OOD methodology guidelines might provide additional assurance of specification correctness prior to the possibility of performing any programming in lower-level languages. Finally, during production operation, the maintenance staff will have access to computer-aided documentation that will provide the same easy modifiability that it did during prototype iteration.

CASE TOOL SHORTCOMINGS

An understanding of common weaknesses found in many CASE products will perhaps be helpful for comparing products prior to an acquisition. The most important weakness to understand is the drawing deficiencies. Often there is a significant delay (several seconds) between the time the user commands a change to the drawing and the time the change appears on the screen. This is most often due to the fact that a multi-user repository is being updated. The changes are being written to a complex data management system. This excuse, although understandable, is not acceptable. A computer-aided drawing tool must be at least as fast to use as pencil and paper.

Another factor at work in the selling (or overselling) of object-oriented CASE is market economics. The market for personal computer drawing tools is vastly larger than the market for CASE tools. Thus, comparatively large efforts have gone into understanding what users want, in terms of the look, feel, and operation of the PC-based drawing tools. If CASE vendors were smart, they would extend this look and feel into their products, but they often don't.

A common weakness of CASE products is their lack of adequate report-generation capability. Again, the CASE vendors could benefit greatly by studying how related PC-based products, such as database management systems and many project management systems, provide this functionality. Virtually every popular PC database product has an easy-to-use, flexible report writer that allows the user to create reports selected and formatted in any manner desired without having to do any programming. Since a CASE tool is essentially a specialized type of data repository, why aren't there better CASE report-writer modules that would allow analysts and designers to create customized requirements and design specifications according to whatever tailored version of whatever documentation format they are using on their project? Instead, we get inflexible templates for standard formats such as MIL-STD 2167A, and graphics that are, for some strange inexplicable reason, difficult to transform into figures in the specification. CASE vendors seem to have forgotten that the primary objective of analysis and design is to produce a specification document.

Another common weakness of CASE tools is their inability to keep up with changes in the methodology they support. Developers of methodologies are continually making refinements to the guidelines and notation. This requires the vendor of a CASE tool that supports the modified methodology to make changes to their software. Many of the more popular methodologies are modified every six to twelve months and most software developers have difficulty coming up with new versions of their products that frequently on a sustained basis. This is why we saw tools that mainly supported flow charts when dataflow diagrams were becoming the most prevalent approach to analysis. When the industry had mostly accepted the DeMarco approach to structured analysis, the CASE tools were mostly supporting Gane and Sarsen structured analysis. By the time vendors had switched to DeMarco, analysts wanted to do Ward/Mellor real-time structured analysis. Many of the leading Case tool products were becoming old by software standards (over five years) by the time they offered good support for Ward/Mellor. This meant that they were probably becoming extremely difficult to modify (most were probably written using a hierarchical, procedural approach with a third-generation language). Therefore, when analysis changed again, first to information engineering and then to object-oriented, the old software, in most instances, failed to keep up. This made room for a whole new crop of products that had never been anything but object-oriented. But, as soon as those products became available, the rules and notational conventions for object-oriented analysis changed. This cycle seems to be immutable and one of the tragic flaws of CASE tools.

One final word about keeping up with the methodology. A relatively recent strategy that attempts to solve this problem is the development of CASE tools by the methodologist for the methodology they support. Peter Coad's company produces and sells a CASE tool; OMTool™ was developed at GE to support the Rumbaugh method. Grady Booch, Tony Wasserman, and Ivar Jacobson, all famous and popular object-oriented methodologists, have tools to support their methods. Obviously, this is becoming a somewhat standard approach. The idea is that the methodologist will have the next version of the CASE tool ready to ship concurrently with the next version of the methodology it supports. This is a nice theory, but there are some flaws in the application. First, if the methodology, along with the tool, is proprietary (textbooks and training are only available to purchasers of the software), this will limit use of the methodology and therefore make it not the wisest choice for the analyst. Also, good methodologists are not necessarily the best software developers. In the case of one methodologist, the drawing features of his company's CASE tool suffer a bit in comparison to his fine approach to object-oriented analysis and design.

The best bet is to keep the decisions of which methodology to use separate from which CASE tool to use. Let applications (systems under construction) drive decisions about what methods and techniques to select for the job, and in turn, let the methods and techniques drive decisions about what tools to purchase. So often, that important order of events is reversed. Selecting a tool first and then deciding what applications can be built with it is limiting (when you have a hammer, every problem looks like a nail). Always pick a methodology that is described in a book that can be obtained in any good technical library. Then pick the best CASE tool that supports that methodology.

Another weakness of CASE tools is the consistency-checking that justifies their use over computer-aided drawing tools. There seem to be tools of just two types with respect to consistency-checking. The first type does almost nothing in terms of consistency-checking and is, therefore, little more than an expensive drawing tool. The other type does an overwhelming abundance of consistency-checking. The smallest set of models will cause the latter type of tool to generate many boring pages of consistency checks, mostly trivial and sometimes even erroneous. Of course, most tools allow consistency-checking to be optional. The problem is that searching through the trivial and wrong errors for the important errors can be so tedious that it often makes the whole feature of automated consistency-checking virtually worthless. It is usually more efficient to subject models to peer review, providing at least some element of reasonableness. CASE software with overblown consistency-checking is little more than an expensive drawing tool.

Finally, there is the universal absence of strong coupling between the models and the software application developed from the models. With all this automation and the high price tags, doesn't it seem like there should be some way of guaranteeing, or at least checking, that the application does what the models claim it does? Actually, this may be too difficult for vendors to create in the form of an affordable product. Vendors have been taking the approach of code generation, but we have already pointed out the fallacy of this approach. It may be a nice feature to use once in a while, but it will not guarantee consistency between code and model. We know of one vendor who has a product that can digest C++ and Smalltalk and produce Coad/Yourdon diagrams, but it is strictly a *reverse-engineering* tool and has little in the way of support for analysis and design. Perhaps a tool such as this could be used in combination with an OOA/OOD CASE tool, but that could be awkward. Would convergence of the two models ever be achieved? No tool that we know of simply looks at the source code and produces a listing of consistency errors in comparison with the models. What would be wrong with that approach, if it was accurate, reasonable, and not overblown?

PROPOSED DIRECTIONS FOR FUTURE CASE TOOL DEVELOPMENT

We often advocate the use of CASE tools to our clients, while counseling caution in terms of expectations and usage. We do not have an absolute favorite, as there are many worthwhile products available. Every software project and particularly every object-oriented rapid prototyping project should have one of these products. The following features are what we would like to see in the next generation of CASE tools so that OOA/OOD may be adequately supported.

Vendors would be smart to spend more programming effort on making drawing tools more like those found in good personal computer drawing packages such as Canvas™ from Deneba. Drawing commands should be completely mouse, tool pallet, and menu driven—no cryptic alphanumeric commands, and no having to guess which mouse button to click. Of course, excellent on-line help facilities are required. Follow the rules for good GUI—MicroSoft and Apple have spent millions on psychological studies, and many of those studies are published in the open literature. The analyst should not have to think any more about the use of a drawing tool than he or she would about the use of a plastic template and mechanical pencil. It should be intuitive and not require hours of studying of the manual or a training course. The user should be able to start drawing models within minutes of taking the shrinkwrap off your product.

Users should be allowed to define their own graphical notational conventions to represent the components (objects, processes, data stores, dataflows, messages, instance connections, etc.) of the methodology. Internal to vendor software is a mapping between the shape the user draws and the methodology component the shape represents. Capability should be provided that allows this mapping to be modified by the user. If, for instance, an object is represented by a box with rounded corners, the user should be able to command that henceforth, objects be represented by square boxes or circles or clouds or whatever shape is desired. Then the tool would know to generate the new shape whenever the user wants a new object. This modifiable shape mapping feature would go a long way toward allowing users to customize the tool in order to help it keep up with methodology changes.

The problem with generating custom reports could easily be fixed with the standard data export features found in most good personal computer packages. Drawings, data dictionaries, method, module, or service specifications should all be exportable in formats usable by other desktop software. Then the user could pick up the data with a favorite database, word processor, spreadsheet, or desktop publishing package, format the document, and print out whatever type of document is required. This type of export feature would be effort much better spent than trying to develop the most excellent report writer or the most wonderful set of standard specification templates. There is no such thing as standard specification formats, because software developers always tailor the standard format they are using for each new project.

An expert system for allowing power users to add their own consistency-checking rules and to specify which rules are to be checked against which models would be extremely valuable.

Tools to generate code that is tightly coupled to analysis/design models will be expensive to develop. What is needed is an executable, interpreted, high-level scripting language that the analyst can use to write service specifications from within the CASE tool (e.g., the pseudo-code-like language provided by Information Engineering Facility™, a CASE tool from Texas Instruments), coupled somehow with an object-oriented GUI builder, such as XVT. There would also have to be good debugging tools for the scripting language. Then when prototype and model are approved, at the end of prototype iteration, an automatic translator should be available to translate the service specification scripts into C++ or Smalltalk, automatically encapsulated with their specified attributes in their specified objects.

Vendors should survey their requirements commissioners (potential customers) to gather requirements and find out what is really wanted and needed. Vendors, anxious to expound upon expectations of sales for the next quarter, frequently hold closed product presentations at their facilities. Developers should not assume that invitations to those meetings implies an opportunity to provide feedback. Too often, the product is already developed and potential users become the unwitting testers. Requirements commissioners of the CASE tool should be shown prototype iterations during the early stages of requirements analysis, not during beta test.

A SHORT TAXONOMY OF EXISTING TOOLS

Figure 11.1 shows some of our favorite products. We have used each of these products on various object-oriented rapid prototyping projects and can recommend all of them as worth their price. Any of these products will provide a net productivity gain that will justify their expense. The column headings are the features we think should be evaluated in each CASE product. The number of symbols in each cell represent how the product in that row ranks, in our opinion, on the feature in that column. We evaluate drawing tools on the basis of ease of use and methodology intelligence (ability to save drawing time through knowledge of the methodology's graphic notation). OOA/OOD support is an evaluation of the tool's ability to support a methodology compatible with object-oriented rapid prototyping. As we have indicated, our preferences for OOA/OOD are Coad/Yourdon, Rumbaugh, Booch, Jacobson, or Wirff-Brock. For this feature, we are looking primarily at the goodness of consistency-checking. Extendibility is evaluated on the basis of how easy it is to use the tool for purposes beyond those it was designed for—a new version of an existing supported methodology, or a new methodology. Can the graphic notation and or the consistency rules be modified by the user? Does the tool allow for workarounds, using annotations or some other device? Report formatting is evaluated on the ease of creating specification documents in custom, user-defined formats. The sparseness of the matrix is an indication of our feeling that these products should offer a lot more value for the money they cost.

Teamwork™ by Cadre is a mature suite of very expensive tools

Product	Drawing Tools	OOA/OOD Support	Extendabillity	Report Formatting
Teamwork	●	●	● ●	● ●
STP	● ●	●	● ●	● ●
Deft	● ● ●	●	● ●	● ●
TurboCase	● ● ●	● ● ● ●	● ●	● ●
CRC Cards	● ● ●	● ●	●	● ●
Mac Analyst	● ● ●	● ● ●	● ●	● ●
OOA Tool	● ●	● ● ● ● ● ●	●	● ●
Object Modeler	● ● ● ●	● ● ● ●	● ●	● ● ● ● ●
MacDraw	● ● ● ●		● ● ● ● ●	

Figure 11.1: Good object-oriented CASE tools

for Unix workstations and IBM PCs running OS/2. The lineage goes all the way back to DeMarco structured analysis, includes Yourdon/Constantine structured design, Ward/Mellor and Hatley/Phirbai real-time structured analysis, and Schlaer/Mellor object-oriented analysis and design. Some users feel that drawing with Teamwork is somewhat awkward. There is no Coad/Yourdon support, and the consistency-checking against supported methodologies may be considered excessive. Customization is through a utility called Access℗ and involves C programming. It is possible, but not easy. Some extendibility exists simply because there is such a large tool suite that, if given all the modules, a workaround may be developed. We have used Teamwork, with some difficulty, to develop Coad/Yourdon models. Document formatting is provided through a set of standard specification templates, including DOD standard 2167A. If the data is desired in any other format, the user must return to Access and C programming again.

STP℗ stands for Software Through Pictures from Interactive Development Environment (IDE). STP is similar to Teamwork, with the exception of the Access tool and support for Schlaer/Mellor OOA and OOD. STP is targeted at the Unix workstation market. We have successfully used workarounds with the real-time structured analysis tools to do Coad/Yourdon OOA and OOD using STP. IDE wants the user to adopt their proprietary methodology and CASE product—object-oriented structured design. This tool cannot be used to support any of the good, publicly available, widely used methodologies. IDE has recently purchased OMTool℗ to support Rumbaugh's method developed at GE.

Deft℗ is a Macintosh-based tool sold by Sybase. It is a structured analysis tool with very strong support for data modeling. The data modeling tools make it possible to use, with workarounds, for most of the referenced OOA/OOD methods. The drawing tools, because they are mostly adherent to the standard Macintosh look and feel, are more acceptable than those found in Teamwork or STP. It will still be difficult to produce an attractive report or specification document using Deft.

TurboCase,™ from Structsoft, is an almost exact replica of Teamwork, except that it runs on a Macintosh, and Teamwork doesn't. Also, TurboCase provides good support for Coad/Yourdon, including worthwhile consistency checking, and Teamwork doesn't.

CRC Cards™ exist in two versions, both for Macintosh. One is a public domain HyperCard stack, available from many public access bulletin boards and Macintosh user groups. The other is available only by attending Apple Computer's Developer University courses for C++ and Macintosh Programmers Workshop. We wish there were readily available, commercially supported versions of this good tool for all platforms. CRC Cards supports Rebecca Wirff-Brocks' Responsibility-Driven Design approach and could also be used effectively for support of any of the referenced OOA/OOD methods. It is really easy to use and generates nice C++ or Smalltalk classes. It does not do drawings. Each card (screen) represents an object and contains information about connections between objects. A collection of cards is logically, but not visually, equivalent to an object class diagram.

Mac Analyst™ is fairly equivalent to TurboCASE, except it does not do as good a job of implementing Coad/Yourdon support. There are some serious inaccuracies. It runs on Macs only.

Object Tool™ is produced and distributed by Peter Coad's organization, Object International. The first version of this product was referred to as OOA Tool. It runs under Unix, Mac, and Microsoft Windows. Support of the Coad/Yourdon methodology is expectably excellent. The biggest weakness is in the awkwardness of the drawing tools as mentioned earlier.

Our *best pick* object-oriented CASE tool at the time of this writing is Object Modeler™ from Iconix. We have used both the Macintosh and Unix versions. They are easy to draw with, and data can be easily exported to word processing and desktop publishing packages when it is time to produce a specification. Support for the most current version of the Coad/Yourdon methodology is almost correct. Other popular OOA and OOD methodologies are also supported such as Booch and Jacobson. Object Modeler is priced very reasonably at less than half of the nearest competitive product. The few weaknesses that exist are minor.

Clearly, this list omits many excellent tools. Our point is that object-oriented CASE tools may be employed to speed the rapid prototyping process, sometimes in addition to the OORP tools discussed in Chapter 4.

12

Documentation

There is good news for organizations having strict documentation standards—object-oriented rapid prototyping provides a way to produce specification documents for a fraction of the effort normally spent. On the other hand, organizations having no documentation requirements will find that OORP provides a means of producing specifications that is so low in effort and so significant in productivity improvement that it is a welcomed fringe benefit. An increase in productivity gained from having simple, graphic descriptions of how the evolving prototype works is always a bonus. The amount of documentation produced should always be the same—the minimum amount that is actually useful and will yield a net productivity gain during development. Good documentation is a by-product that will serve the system during the entire lifecycle, particularly in the expensive maintenance phase, which continues long after the development phase is over.

This chapter provides a cookbook approach to developing good deliverable software specifications with minimum effort. Every object-oriented rapid prototyping project should produce functional specifications (i.e., a requirements document), design specifications, a user guide, and test documentation. Each of these documents can be started concurrently as part of the development of the very *first* version of the prototype. The formal process for prototype iteration explained in this book then provides a way to treat deliverables as living documents, expanding and refining them with each version of the prototype.

FORMATTING ISSUES

Organizations requiring formal documentation typically have standards to which the documents must conform. Many times these standards are based on frameworks that are used by other organizations doing the same kind of work. For instance, MIL-STD 2167A is a framework for DoD software development; NASA Software Documentation Standards are used by NASA contractors; and IEEE-1074 is available from the Technical Committee on Software Engineering of the IEEE Computer Society at nominal cost. Commercial products such as SDM-Structured and PRISM® are used widely by IS organizations. Most software developers today work in organizations that require use of a framework straight from the literature, or one that has been tailored specifically for the locality. Few reinvent the wheel, but draw upon standards that have proved useful elsewhere.

Most process frameworks require developers to produce a software requirements document, preliminary design document, detailed design document, test documentation such as a plan and results, and a user guide. There are variations in these names from one framework to another, and there are formats, or templates, for many more kinds of documents; this is simply the minimum set. A valid reason for using such frameworks is to ensure that the content of the specifications is similar across many projects in large organizations and across many organizations with a single large customer such as NASA.

Many development efforts, however, do not occur in organizations as large as NASA. In companies where each individual project may be viewed as small, the company as a whole manages a portfolio of projects and can greatly benefit from consistency in documentation. Probably nothing else can contribute so handily to the communication among projects or to the communication between the developer and maintainer as a common language provided by consistent documentation. To accomplish this, paragraph headers for all the main sections and subsections are provided in a template. An additional guide, called a content guide, provides generic, high-level descriptions of the type of content to be provided and frequently accompanies the guide with a typical example.

A difficulty of these frameworks is that they typically lag behind state-of-the-art and even state-of-the-practice by a decade or more. None of the current frameworks are really suitable for object-oriented rapid prototyping. Fortunately, most groups encourage developers to tailor the document formats for each project. Tailoring can be mutually agreed upon by the developer and requirements commissioner organizations and a new format can be forged. Suggested formats are offered in this chapter.

Another difficulty of existing format frameworks is that they tend to encourage the expenditure of far too much effort on documentation. Specification of too many different kinds of documents and requirements for too much content to be rendered in nothing more specific than narrative prose is fuel for overkill. Sometimes, overformalization is used for little other than satisfaction of the auditors. A golden opportunity to double software development productivity in many large bureaucratic organizations may be seized by simply applying common sense to the documentation issue.

For example, many currently used templates for the Requirements document have a section for specifying functions and a separate section for data specifications. Putting object services in the functional section and object attributes in the data section runs counter to the principles of encapsulation. We recommend a tailoring that combines these two sections of existing frameworks into a single section, titled, for example, "Data and Functional Requirements." The object class model should appear at the front of this section and provide the primary focus of the section. Major paragraphs in the section would be the specifications of the object classes. For each object, there would be subparagraphs to specify services and attributes.

CONTENT ISSUES

Given a document format, the contents of the documents to be produced must be altered to allow for the products of an OORP project. The following paragraphs give formats, or templates, for requirements and design documents, user guide, and test documentation, and suggest content for each. Of course, any project-specific format framework may have requirements for many more documents. Keep in mind, however, that adding more documents may lead to overspecification. Resist the urge to include more than is necessary and useful.

Within each of the formats below, there is a description of how the natural outputs of a rapid prototyping project might fit into these new frameworks. It takes a bold approach to tailor existing frameworks and to use the following content-to-format mappings; these descriptions will appear radical to some.

OBJECT-ORIENTED REQUIREMENTS SPECIFICATION PRODUCED USING RAPID PROTOTYPING

The Requirements Specification document will likely contain the source/sink diagram and the object class model as graphic representations. In addition, the Requirements Specification Document may appropriately contain some high-level specifications, such as names of objects, services, and attributes. These things will change as a result of prototype iterations, so there will always be two versions of the Requirements Specification—before and after prototype iteration. The portion of the overall Requirements Specification that contains the graphical models must be under some type of configuration management system, or at minimum, be a changeable component. The models undergo continuous evolution and refinement during prototype iteration, while the Requirements Specification document itself may contain descriptive text that is fairly stable—changed and republished only at major review points. Because of their volatility, it is acceptable to refrain from putting service specifications in the Requirements Specification Document and hold them for inclusion in the Preliminary Design Document. The timing may be better since detailed software requirements cannot be really known until the end of prototype iteration.

Referenced Documents

If the format framework requires a section containing referenced documents, this is where the name of the framework in use may be revealed. Methodology texts should also be listed, as some readers of the Requirements Specification Document may be unfamiliar with the notational conventions of the chosen models.

Examples of such texts include *Object-Oriented Analysis,*[1] *Structured Rapid Prototyping,*[2] *Designing Object-Oriented Software,*[3] *Software Requirements: Analysis and Specification,*[4] *Structured Analysis,*[5] *and System Specification, Specifications for Real-Time Systems Analysis,*[6] and this text.

Interface Requirements

Some frameworks call for a separate Interface Control Document (ICD) to contain interface requirements. Others, such as NASA Software Documentation Standards, allow the encapsulation of interface requirements in the main requirements document. We prefer the latter approach because it is sufficient, requires less effort, and leads to less redundancy. Tailor frameworks requiring an ICD to eliminate over-specification.

External Interfaces

The source/sink diagram is the appropriate figure to be included in the first major paragraph of this section entitled External Interfaces. The accompanying descriptive text can simply restate what the diagram shows, for example, "The *objectName* object class shall receive *dataflowName* data from the *sourceName* external entity" and "The *objectName* object class shall issue *dataflowName* data to the *destinationName*. external entity." The dataflows themselves can be rigorously defined in a data dictionary, the next major paragraph. The source/sink diagram was described in Chapter 4.

Preliminary Data Dictionary

Data requirements (attributes) are covered under object class specifications below. In older specification formats, a Data Dictionary was where the decomposition of all the dataflows within the system was defined. Within object-oriented systems, data does not flow, it is encapsulated and thus is appropriately specified as attributes of object classes. As a rule, attributes are atomic, not decomposable.

There are exceptions: external interface dataflows shown on the source/sink diagram may decompose into sets of data elements. Some of these external dataflows may be created by older non-object-oriented systems. Some may be conventional file structures. The Data Dictionary in the Requirements Specification Document should do a good job of defining the components and structure of external dataflow interfaces in order to help developers deal with them. External dataflows represent the mission of a system: to capture the specified inputs from the specified sources outside the boundaries of this system and deliver the specified outputs to the specified destinations outside the boundaries of this system. So that inputs may be properly transformed into outputs, it is extremely important that they are clearly understood. The Preliminary Data Dictionary should be mercifully brief, but may not be eliminated due to its critical nature.

Internal Interfaces

The object class model, defined in Chapter 4, is the appropriate figure for this paragraph of the interface requirements section. It shows the interfaces between internal object classes as instance connections. The accompanying descriptive text can once again simply restate what the diagram shows, providing narrative explanation of the instance connection rules, for example, "For each instance of objectA, there must be at least one and perhaps many instances of objectB." If Rumbaugh is used, links and associations may be named on the object class model, and those names may need further explanation in this section.

Because the primary components of the Interface Requirements section are graphic models along with some very brief, unambiguous, descriptive text, the interface requirements are specified with far less work than that required to produce a traditional interface control document.

Object Class Requirements

There should be a paragraph describing attributes and encapsulated services for each object class in the application system. These paragraphs belong in a section called "Data and Functional Requirements," "Technical Requirements," or, perhaps best of all, "Object Class Requirements". Attributes can simply be listed for each object. Detailed technical attribute definitions with data formats should be saved for the design document. Service specifications can be provided as subparagraphs for each object class.

Service Specifications

It is a challenge to write service specifications for an object-oriented rapid prototype and avoid overspecification. Very quickly at the beginning of the project, scripts will appear in very high-level languages that are devoid of procedural complexity and are very easy to understand. What added value will service specifications provide? For very good prototyping languages, the answer might be, "not much." In this case, it is perfectly acceptable to simply copy the actual scripts into these subparagraphs. They will certainly be nonambiguous.

What about prototyping languages that are just a bit on the side of nonintuitive compared to plain conversational language? Then it may be necessary to provide a simplified interpretation of what the service does, at least in the final requirements document. However, every effort should be made to keep it unambiguous. It is possible to provide less detail than appears in the actual script and increase understandability at the same time. Terse bullet lists of functions performed are a good technique—"the *serviceName* service shall perform the following functions:" followed by the bullet list. If the service only performs a single simple function, such as generating a message when a button is clicked by the user, then a single sentence is sufficient for the service specification.

Control Requirements

Conventional requirements documents do not always contain control requirements. Real-time systems sometimes have state transition diagrams as part of their requirements specifications, yet actual control of program execution is often thought of as a design issue. This thinking needs to be reversed in object-oriented software engineering. Objects have requirements to provide their services when the appropriate message is issued. The understanding of which services are provided in response to which messages is appropriately part of the object-oriented requirements specification. The appropriate figure for this section of the requirements document is the object control matrix defined in Chapter 4. Again, accompanying text describes what the diagram shows—that specified services execute when they trap the occurrence of specified messages. A more specific and detailed message dictionary can be provided in the design document.

Other Requirements—the -*ilities*

Some formatting templates contain paragraphs for many other kinds of requirements. These other requirements are often referred to as the -*ilities* because many of them end in "-ility": quality, maintainability, security, reliability, portability, safety, efficiency, testability, understandability, modifiability, and so forth. We include performance requirements in this group, even though these words do not end in "-ility." Unfortunately these requirements are often stated in narrative prose and read like the proverbial Victorian novel. Developers frequently write that the software will be of high quality, easy to maintain, highly secure, very reliable, extremely portable, very safe, and exceedingly fast—fuzzy requirements that are subject to interpretations and dependencies. The spirit of quality intended by the -ilities requires these words to be more rigorously defined. Ultimately, -ilities must conform to industry expert Barry Boehm's suggestion that all requirements must be quantifiable and testable so that developers can know whether or not they are actually met in the incarnation of the software.

Despite developer efforts to write rigorous specifications, the requirements commissioners will determine degree of satisfaction based on their interpretations and expectations during the evaluation of the actual software performance. It is better for developers to spend effort with the manifestation of these elements in the prototype, since no amount of rigorous documentation can salvage one misinterpretation of expectations.

The amount of detail necessary to describe quality via the -*ilities* will depend on the specific application and on what the requirements commissioners insist on seeing in the specification. A requirements specification that contained no -*ilities* would be adequate, if users were totally satisfied with them as represented in the final version of the prototype.

Preliminary Requirements (versus Final Requirements)

On a rapid prototyping project there should always be at least two deliverable versions of the Requirements Specification Document—preliminary and final. The first version should be very brief, using the same format as that given above, but providing sparse content.

As stated above, the Interface Requirements section should contain only the source/sink diagram, the preliminary Data Dictionary, and the object class model. The formalism of accompanying descriptive text is unnecessary at this point. Since little knowledge of requirements is needed to get started prototyping, these initial models can be very small and intentionally incomplete (maybe a dozen objects or so). If the object classes on the object class model show attributes and services for each, this is sufficient specification for the prototype, and the object class requirements section can be left TBD (to be defined) in this Preliminary Requirements Specification Document. On the other hand, if it is useful to write simple service specifications for complex prototype scripts (we have known several prototypers who did), then by all means do so. But it is best not to get carried away with specifying things that are initially unknown, or unnecessary rework will be created. The object control matrix should be placed in the Control Requirements section and, again, the descriptive text left out. The Other Requirements section (-*ilities*) may be left until publication of the final requirements, or it can be used as a place to capture notes taken during initial user interviews, regarding issues such as performance and security. Whatever is written here will be difficult to criticize or defend as to correctness and completeness, as more project knowledge, to unfold with each prototype version, is needed.

The purpose of the Preliminary Requirements Specification Document is only to provide a guide for prototype development. The prototype itself is not supposed to be complete or correct. There is no need to provide a lot of detail that may be changed by feedback from prototype demonstrations. The Preliminary Requirements Specification Document need only be about six standard $8\frac{1}{2}$ x 11-inch pages in length.

AN OBJECT-ORIENTED DESIGN DOCUMENT

For OORP, the design is inherent in the Preliminary Requirements Specification Document. The prototyper can spot the object classes to be included in the initial prototype. Even the design objects (such as those that implement the user interface) are usually visible. What they contain, what they do, how they are connected to each other, and how they will be controlled are facts available for inclusion in the initial prototype. This is concurrent software engineering. At some point, however, it will be useful to put some of the more detailed implementation-dependent specifications in a separate Design Document, probably at the end of prototype iteration, when all of the implementation details are known. That is why we call the activity *design derivation*. The detailed implementation specification is documentation of the existing, user-approved, final version of the prototype. Because this document only needs to include the additional implementation detail (things that should not be specified until prototype iteration is finished), the Design Document can be much smaller than the final Requirements Specification Document on an object-oriented rapid prototyping project.

Referenced Documents Again

As with the Requirements Specification Document, formal design templates may also require a section containing referenced documents. The requirement is an outgrowth of older methodologies where models and their rule set were different in analysis than in design. For example, traditional structured methods saw the models move from dataflow diagrams in analysis to architecture diagrams in architectural design and then to structure charts (via transform or transaction analysis) in design. Object-oriented rapid prototyping projects are different—the models get refined with each process phase, but they retain the same graphical format. An object class model may have more objects added to it in design, but there is no transition to a completely different format. Often a simple backward reference to the Requirements Specification Document is sufficient, or an electronic copy and paste of the models from a requirements document to a design document.

Software and Hardware Architecture

During the tuning phase, object classes may be distributed among multiple processors across a local or even a wide area network to obtain better performance. Some of the prototype services written in a high-level scripting language may be replaced with more efficient programs written in a lower-level language, as another performance tuning technique. The physical description of what goes where and how it is all connected needs to be specified in the design document in this software/hardware architecture section. Begin, as always with a diagram, but instead of developing a new kind of architecture diagram, simply reuse the object class model. Annotate the final version of this model, as it appears in the Requirements Specification Document, with the application's software and hardware architecture. Next to each object class, specify the language it is written in and the processor upon which the object will reside. Next to instance connections, provide annotations that specify the network protocols, gateways, routers, and bus types (where appropriate) where connections are between objects on different processors.

Detailed Design Data Dictionary—Attribute Definitions

In the data dictionary syntax, object class attribute definitions are simply comments with no particular standard notational convention necessary. In an object-oriented design, there are not hierarchies of dataflow decomposition, as would be seen in a structured design, so an elaborate, complex data dictionary, with special dictionary syntax conventions, is unnecessary. In a structured design data dictionary, the lowest level of the decomposition is the data element, which is equivalent to a field in a file or a variable in a program. Object-oriented software engineering goes directly to this level by encapsulating attributes (the object-oriented equivalent of a data element) in object classes.

Since the Requirements Specification Document contained a preliminary Data Dictionary where attributes were identified but left undefined, the detailed design Data Dictionary becomes the vehicle to flesh out those attributes with technical definitions. It reveals the length, type, and format of each variable, providing adequate maintenance documentation. The data structure of the application appears all in one place and spares the maintainer having to look through the source listings of each object class.

Message Dictionary—Message Specifications

As with the Data Dictionary, messages are not fully defined in the Requirements Specification Document; they are intentionally kept at a high level because details change dynamically during prototype iteration and tuning. The final detailed design is the appropriate place for complete message specification, because messages reflect how the system works (a design issue), rather than what it does (a requirements issue). Of course, with concurrent software engineering it is perfectly acceptable to create a preliminary Message Dictionary during prototype iteration, where all of the system's messages are tracked and gradually refined.

The Message Dictionary can simply be an alphabetized list of message templates. The same information is specified for each message, calling for a standard template:

- Message name
- Source that generates the message
- Condition required in order for message to be generated
- Data passed from source (parameter list)
- Data to be returned to the source (parameter list)

Providing the object control matrix as a figure in this section will give the reader a frame of reference that will make it easy to understand which objects trap which messages, then execute the indicated services, receiving data in the message parameters from the source, and returning data in other parameters to the source.

Detailed Service Specifications

In the Design Document, the service specifications should be very precise and specific, accurately documenting the actual code. As with the Data Dictionary, the objective is to have all documentation needed for maintenance located in one place and not scattered through myriad source code listings. If the scripting language is nonprocedural and very much like conversational language (the best ones are), it is still perfectly acceptable to simply copy the actual scripts into the subparagraphs of this section, keeping in mind that maintenance and configuration management of the documentation must accompany maintenance of the code. Object classes will be the main paragraph headings and their service specifications will be their subparagraphs.

For tuning purposes, object classes may be rewritten in lower-level languages, or primary processing may be replaced with the invocation of an external procedure written in a lower-level language. In these cases thorough documentation of what the service does should be documented in pseudo code. Using the nonprocedural script of the prototype as pseudo code for a procedural program written in a lower-level language will probably not work. It might work, however, if the tuning language is Smalltalk, C++, or some other object-oriented language and the new code is to be written in a nonprocedural, object-oriented fashion.

Performance Requirements

This section of the Design Document should more properly be called "Performance Constraints" or "Performance Attributes". Faster is usually better, all other things being equal, and some responses are just too late to be of any use. Yet, there is an obvious trade-off between functionality and performance. Writing performance requirements such as "All services must complete execution within 10 milliseconds," or "All queries must return results within .5 seconds," may artificially constrain functionality, eliminating the possibility of some useful features. Sometimes the absolute constraint is just a guess and users can comfortably live with slower performance than anticipated.

Our philosophy is that it's better to find out what the requirements commissioners want first, then find out how fast you can give it to them. Ed Yourdon suggested years ago that it is best to make the system "right" before making it "fast." Find out if what's "right" is fast enough, and determine, during the tuning phase, what to do if it's not. In meeting critical performance constraints, some features may be eliminated as a last resort. However, if constraints are found in the requirements document before there is a full understanding of tradeoffs, important functionality may be needlessly sacrificed. A Performance Requirements section in the requirements document would be acceptable only if requirements commissioners agree to keep this section TBD until the start of the tuning phase, after prototype iteration is finished.

Other Design Constraints

There may be other constraints related to the culture and environment in which the application must run. Examples are the brand of computer to be used, final implementation language, and operating system. Often these seem like religious issues because the arguments over which is best may be heated, for no apparently logical reasons. There are, however, some real issues related to compatibility with existing systems and potential conversion and support costs. The decisions about these things often impact many of the other aspects of a system. For instance, the choice of computer, operating system, and development language often has more impact on the look and feel of the application's user interface than anything the developer might do. So, even with object-oriented rapid prototyping, the user may get close to having *anything* he or she wants, but can rarely have *everything* he or she wants within the bounds of design constraints. These constraints and the rationale surrounding the user's choice should be documented for those who follow to maintain the application.

OBJECT-ORIENTED TEST PROCEDURES
AND TEST RESULTS DOCUMENTATION

Test plans and test cases for conventionally developed procedural software are difficult to write.[7,8] With procedural software, there is a very large number of different possible paths through the many different branches within the program logic. Combinations and permutations of data values and decision choices may approach the infinite in large systems. Often the data values processed as input will send the system down different paths, causing the interim and output results to be very different—not always what is expected or desired. A good test plan takes this into account and lays out a strategy for exercising the system to give expected results, given strategically designed test input data that is only a small subset of possible data. Of course, there is a remaining problem that it is never feasible, within schedule and budget, to test as many of the possible different execution variations as desired, and one of the untested paths may well be the first to execute when the system is put into production, perhaps with disastrous results. The fact that the Reliability Requirements section of (an optional document) other requirements within the Requirements Specification says this is not allowed is no help at all.

With object-oriented rapid prototyping, there is a simple, expedient answer to this dilemma. Thanks to encapsulation and the development of a nonprocedural, message-based system, there will no branches or logic paths from the overall system view. Well-designed object classes can be independently tested and will perform exactly the same when integrated with other object classes. Range of value testing is still a necessary activity, but it should really be part of prototype iteration.[9] System profile testing may also be useful.[10] Educate the requirements commissioners to enquire about what happens to services if different data values are input into the attributes or through message parameters. Put plans for showing these what-if scenarios into prototype demonstration scripts. Then, write down the results at the demonstration. The results, at the end of prototype iteration, is a deliverable test plan and test results with little effort, and none beyond what is needed for good prototyping anyway. Of course, if this utopian environment is upset by the addition of conventional procedural software during tuning, all of the problems of test planning identified above will resurface, and the test plan will have to be modified. Tuned services may need to be tested according to conventional unit testing rules.[11,12]

USER GUIDES

Strange as it may sound, we believe that the best user guide is none at all. When the developer does an exemplary job of prototyping the user interface, the need for a lengthy user guide (explaining in laborious detail the arcane workings of a user-hostile interface) just isn't necessary. Ideally, the prototyped application will be so intuitive and self-explanatory, that a new user can be up to speed and fully productive within moments of first introduction to the software. The danger here is in the very concept of a *new* user.

During prototype iteration, it is probable that a small subset of the universe of all possible future users of the application is becoming intimately familiar with all of the inner workings of the software—including its difficulties. It is good to develop help screens as part of the prototype, as previously mentioned. But users will quickly lose interest in these screens after they become familiar with the prototype. We have even seen cases where users demand, in their role as prototype requirements commissioners, that the help buttons be removed from all screens to make room for more features.

Who should be commissioning the requirements for the help features? Not all users; experienced users don't need help. Requirements commissioners for help screens should be brand new users who have never seen the system before. Ask them if help screens are needed, or if the ones that exist are adequate. Find these people and get them involved late in the prototype iteration process, when functionality is nearing completion and the original set of requirements commissioners have become jaded by overfamiliarity.

Without a doubt, the best user guides we have ever seen for commercial software have been ones that are electronic rather than paper-based and are an integral part of the operational application, accessible through a menu pick or the click of a button. Often such help modules are developed with good prototyping tools, such as Gain Momentum, HyperCard or PowerBuilder. Rapid prototyping techniques are often used to ensure that the help is actually helpful. The Help Object from the Gain Momentum bundled object class library and the HyperCard help stack are examples of this—there is no better way to learn Gain Momentum or HyperCard, and reading the paper User Manuals is, comparatively, a waste of time. So, our best advice is, develop an electronic user guide in the form of a Help object class and use rapid prototyping techniques with new users as requirements commissioners to make sure the help is actually helpful. Then, if auditors or management insist on a document, print out all the help screens, bind them into a document and deliver them.

In summary, the above four easy documents are all the documentation you need for any project and can be produced on an OORP project in a fraction of the time required using a more conventional approach!

ENDNOTES

1. Coad, P., and Yourdon, E., *Object-Oriented Analysis*, New York: Yourdon Press (Prentice-Hall), 1991.

2. Connell, J., and Shafer, L., *Structured Rapid Prototyping: An Evolutionary Approach to Software Development*, Englewood Cliffs, NJ: Prentice-Hall, Inc., 1989.

3. Wirff-Brock, R., Wilkerson, B., and Wiener, L., *Designing Object-Oriented Software*, Englewood Cliffs, NJ: Prentice-Hall, Inc., 1990.

4. Davis, A. M., *Software Requirements: Analysis and Specification*, Englewood Cliffs, NJ: Prentice-Hall, Inc., 1990.

5. DeMarco, T., *Structured Analysis and System Specification*, New York: Yourdon Press, 1983.

6. Hatley, R., and Pirbahi, I., *Specifications for Real-Time Systems Analysis*, New York Dorsett House, 1986.

7. IEEE, *Software Test Documentation*, ANSI/IEEE Std 829–1983, New York: IEEE, 1983.

8. IEEE, *Software Verification and Validation Plans*, ANSI/IEEE Std. 1012–1986, New York: IEEE, 1986.

9. Beizer, B., *Software Testing Techniques*, New York: Van Nostrand Reinhold, 1990.

10. Musa, J. D., "Operational Profiles in Software-Reliability Engineering", *IEEE Software*, March 1993, 14–32.

11. McCabe, T. J., *Structured Testing*, Silver Spring, MD: IEEE, 1983.

12. Myers, G. J., *The Art of Software Testing*, New York: John Wiley and Sons, 1979.

13

Startup

Object-oriented rapid prototyping can make organizations more successful, enhance individual careers, and make users happier by providing more useful software applications at a lower price. Whether or not it becomes a mainstream approach to software development in your organization may depend on a grass roots movement. When everyone in an environment agrees about the best approach to software development, benefits of the approach increase significantly. At the same time, it would be useful to know what individuals can do, working alone or with a small team of colleagues, to get things started.

It is improbable that many people in any given organization will agree as to what object-oriented software engineering or rapid prototyping mean. Often, when developers refer to coding without specification as rapid prototyping, they are simply rationalizing shoddy software engineering. The following are some tips to move an organization in the right direction.

THE OWNERS OF THE PROCESS

Who will do object-oriented rapid prototyping—centralized MIS organizations or decentralized projects managed by various user groups? Who will participate in these projects—analysts, developers, or users? Will standards and policies answer these questions, or will each project decide these issues anarchistically? The answers will be different in different organizations. But it is important to recognize that the real owners of any process are those responsible for implementing it. Software development projects are owned by software developers. Users and managers are important stakeholders, but they do not own the process. If requirements commissioners dictate the methods to use, the methods may not be applied successfully unless there is full buy-in on the part of developers. On the other hand, developers can successfully use their favored methods in secret while giving the external appearance of complying with the mandated method. The software developers must be won over before true process improvement can occur.

Centralized prototyping approaches allow for economies of scale, particularly when it comes to sharing the expense of some of the more robust prototyping tools. Centralization also increases the chances of successful object class reuse through properly supported repositories. On the other hand, centralization of software development tends to create an *us-versus-them* feeling between developers and users, creating a distance that can be difficult to bridge during prototyping. What works best is when resources are provided from a central organization but projects are decentralized and under user control. While management debates these issues, each individual may begin to do his or her part.

Rapid prototyping is not a recognized professional skill category. Despite the fact that it is a widely practiced approach, there are not many job advertisements asking for rapid prototyping skills. In a sense, this is unfortunate, since software development organizations are often dependent on their recruiting departments to fill openings. Recruiters usually end up interviewing hordes of C/Unix programmers with Computer Science degrees who may not have been given the opportunity to fully comprehend the complexities of building a system in a team environment so that the system will be efficient and maintainable from inception to obsolescence. They may not have been taught in school how to leverage advanced development environments and concurrent specification approaches to obtain significant productivity improvements. They may have worked only on problems small enough for individuals to solve, not complex enough to require the interactions of a fully functional team.

Rapid prototypers really need skills beyond those of ordinary programmers in areas such as group dynamics, ego suppression, willingness to admit ignorance, empathy with other people's problems, creative laziness, and passion for experimentation. These skills are both rare and valuable, but hard to recruit and sometimes hard to recognize. Human resources departments may be made aware of these facts but they could also use knowledgeable software engineers to take a more active role in the recruiting process. Seasoned prototypers can ask to be allowed to meet candidates for new software developer positions, even if the new hires won't be reporting to them. Candidates can be evaluated on the basis of the above criteria, and feedback provided to management.

THE TOOL BIN

Should each project acquire its own hardware and software to use for rapid prototyping? In the case of object-oriented rapid prototyping, it is very important to do everything possible to encourage reuse of existing object classes made available through a central repository, because object-oriented reuse has more potential for increasing productivity than any other technique. If every project has a different development environment, unique to the project, widespread reuse will not result.

Rather than enforcing standards, central organizations should provide *free,* or attractively priced, access to supported development tools, subsidized with overhead dollars collected from a tax on all projects. This would encourage developers to use the supported tools. If the central organization also provided *free* training and consulting on the use of the tools, this would enhance the choice of the supported tool even more and soon most projects would be using the same tools and contributing new object classes to a repository managed by the central organization. One of the authors manages a central support organization at NASA Ames Research Center that works exactly in this manner, and has found it to be a very effective approach.

One issue regarding centralized tool bins is technical obsolescence. If large investments are made in powerful but expensive rapid prototyping environments, there will be a tendency to delay replacing those tools when more powerful ones are introduced. More powerful rapid prototyping tools are introduced every month, but tool bin contents, obviously, cannot be replaced every month. It simply wouldn't be cost effective to do so, regardless of the productivity improvements to be gained from introduction of the new tools.

The issue of technical obsolesence is one good reason for not setting and enforcing organizational standards regarding approved development environments. Early adapters may determine that, for their project, the benefits to be gained from a new tool outweigh the benefits of free seats, training, and consulting provided with centrally supported tools. If it is true that the new tool is better than the centrally supported tool, everybody wins. The project is more successful than it would have been without the new tool and the central organization obtains a thorough field test of a potential new candidate for the tool bin. In fact, at NASA Ames, rather than resisting such technological change, the central support group employs a New Technology Specialist to seek out new tools, evaluate them, and match them (by recommendation) with early adapters who are looking for improved tools.

Management should be aware that expensive, powerful, rapid prototyping tools are best acquired using overhead funds provided from a tax on all development projects. Prototyping proponents may show managers the benefits by doing successful object-oriented rapid prototyping with the best tools available. Proponents can share the cost of acquiring more expensive tools with other projects, using the potential for enhanced reuse as a motivator. Very small projects, or those with very limited funds, can sometimes get a free ride with a richer project; the disadvantaged project can ask if tools can be shared using the enhanced reuse argument. Then, when enhanced reuse really does happen on all cooperating projects, the measured productivity improvement can be reported to management and the lobby for central support for tools can be continued.

SELLING OBJECT-ORIENTED RAPID PROTOTYPING AS A STANDARD DEVELOPMENT METHODOLOGY

The central support group at NASA Ames has hit on a formula for standardizing projects on a development methodology that appears to be extremely effective. Most new development projects are using OORP and achieving successful results. The formula is similar to the new technology infusion strategy outlined above. As is the case with tools, development methodology standards are supported rather than enforced.

A Software Engineering Guidebook (SEG), available as a contractor's report from any NASA library,[1] was published by the Software Engineering Process Group (SEPG) and distributed to all software developers. The SEG functions as a catalog of development methods supported by the SEPG. A training director, working in the SEPG, puts together courses in all the methods described in the guidebook. Members of the SEPG are often the teachers of these courses. While teaching a course, a support group member will often learn of teams who are considering applying the method being taught to their new development projects. The instructor then offers to personally provide *free* (prepaid) consulting to the project team to help them apply their newly acquired skills to real work. In addition, the group's new technology specialist will provide access to object-oriented rapid prototyping tools, along with consulting and training on use of the tools. It's an approach and a standing offer that has been hard for most projects to resist. It works wonderfully and with each success more projects are interested in jumping on the bandwagon.

Ed Yourdon points out, in *Object-Oriented System Design*,[2] that although object-oriented languages are very popular, object-oriented methods are slower in being widely adopted. He attributes this to the necessity for a paradigm shift—a change in the way developers think about software architecture. New C++ programmers with a C programming background can simply write C++ code that looks like C. Analysts and designers with a structured background have a harder time converting what they know about dataflow and structure chart modeling to object class modeling. Yourdon cites the NASA Ames centrally supported mentoring approach as one good way to help developers through the paradigm shift.

Organizations that are too small, or simply cannot afford such a central support group, may achieve the same goals working as independent agents, while simultaneously lobbying for the formation of such a group. Of course, in these smaller organizations, the support group will be a scaled-down version of the one described above. Upon completion of each successful project, the project members can be advertised as consultants for object-oriented rapid prototyping. Their time may be sold internally, or at a minimum, given away over lunch meetings. In the consulting business, this is known as practice development. Individuals may tell their manager this is what they would like to do with at least part of their time. We can testify that it's enjoyable. It's fun showing others how to be more successful and very satisfying to see the results.

SOFTWARE MAINTENANCE DISAPPEARS AT LAST

Executives don't like spending large portions of their software budgets just to maintain existing software. It is analogous to spending more to maintain a computer (or television set or refrigerator) than it cost to buy in the first place. With today's new object-oriented approach to software development, traditional maintenance is replaced by the addition, modification, and replacement of software components known as object classes. When you buy a new hard disk, or replace your old CPU chip with a faster one, you are upgrading your system, not maintaining it. Modern object-oriented applications are like large computer networks. Components are added, modified, and replaced, but the whole collection of components is almost never thrown away and redeveloped from scratch.

Additions, modifications, and replacements of object class components enhance existing applications rather than fixing things that are broken. With object-oriented rapid prototyping, broken components get fixed during prototype iteration and tend to stay fixed over the life of the product. This is what is meant by the disappearance of software maintenance. To the extent that the existing components were created using advanced rapid prototyping tools and then leveraged into production without being rewritten in a lower-level language, future modifications will be just like another prototype iteration. Post-delivery changes will be just a way to make users happier, instead of high-stress repair work performed in an attempt to keep angry users at bay.

Furthermore, as reuse becomes more practical with the increased growth of good object-oriented repositories, development projects will disappear along with maintenance tasks. All that will be left is modification, replacement, and recombination of existing object classes with, very rarely, the creation of a few new object classes. However, rapid prototyping will still not disappear as an extremely valuable approach. We will still need to determine what the requirements commissioners want from the recombination of added, modified, and replaced object classes. So we will always have rapid prototyping projects; they just won't involve much development from scratch.

Object-oriented rapid prototyping projects of the future will begin most often with a request to upgrade an existing application. Object-oriented analysis will be used to model the enhancements requested. Existing object-oriented analysis and design models will also be reusable and will be stored along with the software in the reuse repository. The new model will most likely consist of object classes of the current application that do not require any changes, existing object classes from the reuse repository that can be used for part of the requested enhancement features, and maybe a few new object classes that do not currently exist. Tools from the tool bin will be used to prototype the new object classes, and the first version of the prototype can be shown to the users the day after the request is received. The whole upgrade project will probably be finished, including final testing, in a few weeks.

Why all this talk of maintenance in a chapter on starting up the object-oriented rapid prototyping approach in an organization? It's important to understand that whatever the type of software task being engaged in at the moment—whether it is called maintenance or development—it is perfectly appropriate to develop an object-oriented rapid prototype of the object classes thought necessary to support the new features. These new objects may then be interfaced to existing software as if the existing software was an external system (show it as such on the source/sink diagram), even if the existing software is the major part of an application to which a minor enhancement is merely being added. For similar reasons, and using similar approaches, it is never too late to introduce object-oriented rapid prototyping on an existing project. Don't wait for the next project—do it now!

WHO PAYS HOW MUCH FOR OBJECT-ORIENTED RAPID PROTOTYPING PROJECTS?

The most sensible way to cost object-oriented rapid prototyping projects is on the basis of number of total objects requested, minus the number of currently existing object classes that can be reused, times an expansion ratio to allow for all the things the requirements commissioners will not think of in the original request but will be discovered and implemented during prototype iterations. An algorithm for this type of estimate was presented in Chapter 10. If large amounts of reuse are possible, showing the subtraction for reuse in the calculation used for the estimate will make very low estimates more believable (and more competitive in proposal situations).

For accurate metrics, estimates of time expected to be spent by requirements commissioners in the tasks of reviewing the prototype and studying the output to determine completeness, correctness, and exactness must be included. They are as much a part of the team and expend effort, the same as all other team members. Requirements commissioners should pay for the applications they request.

Does it make sense to apply object-oriented productivity metrics to your current or next project, even if they are not object-oriented projects and estimates and schedules have already been determined using some other metric, such as lines of code? We think so, because the other metrics are not reliable and are not going to be compatible with an infusion of object-oriented rapid prototyping into the project. It will only take a few hours to generate a simple OOA model, and only a few minutes more to generate new estimates based on object-oriented productivity metrics. Managers need to know the advantage of doing this; proponents of prototyping who are not directed to do so may do it anyway. These metrics will be needed when the creation of a simple, quick, object-oriented rapid prototype is proposed and the "How long will it take?" question is asked.

Good luck and good prototyping! Write us care of the publisher or send e-mail and let us know how you're doing. Clearly, it is one of our favorite subjects and we would like to help if we can. Our Internet addresses are:

connell@george. arc. nasa.gov

lshafer@zilker.net

ENDNOTES

1. Connell, J., and Wenneson, G., *Software Engineering Guidebook*, NASA Contractor's Report, Moffett Field, CA: NASA Ames Research Center, 1993.
2. Yourdon, E., *Object-Oriented System Design*, New York: Yourdon Press (Prentice-Hall, Inc.), 1994.

Acronyms/Abbreviations

AFD: Architecture Flow Diagram
CPU: Central Processing Unit
CRC: Class-Responsibility-Collaborator
CAD: Computer-Aided Design
CASE: Computer-Aided Software Engineering
COCOMO: COnstructive COst MOdel
CFD: Control Flow Diagram
DD: Data Dictionary
DFD: DataFlow Diagram
DMS: Data Management System
DoD: Department of Defense
DOS: Disk Operating System
ERD: Entity-Relationship Diagram
4GL: Fourth Generation Language
GE: General Electric
GUI: Graphical User Interface
IEF: Information Engineering Facility
IDE: Interactive Development Environment
LAN: Local Area Network
MS: Microsoft Windows
MIL-STD: Military Standard
NASA: National Aeronautics and Space Administration
NIH: Not Invented Here
OCM: Object Control Matrix
OMT: Object Modeling Technology
OOA: Object-Oriented Analysis
OODMS: Object-Oriented Data Management System

OOD: Object-Oriented Design
OOEP: Object-Oriented Effort Points
OOPM: Object-Oriented Productivity Metrics
OOP: Object-Oriented Program
OOPL: Object-Oriented Programming Language
OORP: Object-Oriented Rapid Prototype
OOW: Object-Oriented Workstation
ODBC: Open DataBase Concept
PDL: Program Design Language (pseudo-code)
RAD: Rapid Application Development
RISC: Reduced Instruction Set Computing
RDMS: Relational Database Management System
RFP: Request For Proposal
SDK: Software Developer's Kit
SEG: Software Engineering Guidebook
SEPG: Software Engineering Process Group
STP: Software Through Pictures
SLOC: Source Lines Of Code
SA: Structured Analysis
SD: Structured Design
3GL: Third Generation Language
WBS: Work Breakdown Structure
Xerox PARC: Xerox Palo Alto Research Center

Index